MAINTAIN

EYES TO THE RIM

NEVER QUIT ON A PLAY

BBLE A LOOSE BALL

NG ANGLE

STILL CHASING

BALL

CONTEST EVERY SHOT

VE A VERBAL

AIR TIME OF THE BALL

ARE NOISY

FOULING NEGATES HUSTLE

MAKE A[
GET OUT OF THE MUD
DO YOUR JOB
NEVER D[
DRIBBLE TO AN IMPROVED PA[
TURN THE TIDE
VALUE THI[
KNOW YOUR SLIP POINT[
REACH FOR THE LIGHTS   G[
ENDURANCE, VISION, ANTICIPATION & URG[
MOVE ON TH[
GREAT DEFENSE[

To Jon,

A friend who definitely has found his "PURPOSE" in Life!

Thank you for giving me the Confidence + encouragement to write this book when we met in Chicago. You have been an inspiration to me with your Faith, Energy + Positivity!

Thank you for Living your life "ALL IN" for others!

Peter

ALL
IN

DRIVEN BY PASSION, ENERGY, AND PURPOSE

ALL IN

DRIVEN BY PASSION, ENERGY, AND PURPOSE

PORTER MOSER

FOREWORD BY SISTER JEAN DOLORES SCHMIDT, BVM

LOYOLA PRESS.
Chicago

LOYOLA PRESS.

3441 N. Ashland Avenue
Chicago, Illinois 60657
(800) 621-1008
www.loyolapress.com

Cover art credit: Kevin C. Cox/Getty Images Sport/Getty Images.
Dust jacket flap, author photo, Steve Woltmann Photography.

ISBN: 978-0-8294-5001-9
Library of Congress Control Number: 2019954729

Printed in the United States of America.
19 20 21 22 23 24 25 26 27 28 LSC 10 9 8 7 6 5 4 3 2 1

To my parents, Jim and Sandy: thank you for providing me with a childhood of love, life lessons, and the positive belief that I could accomplish anything with faith, energy, and passion.

CONTENTS

FOREWORD

I am Sister Jean Dolores Schmidt, a Sister of Charity of the Blessed Virgin Mary, whose motherhouse is in Dubuque, Iowa. Most people know me simply as Sister Jean. I have been the chaplain for the Loyola Ramblers men's basketball team for more than twenty years, since 1994. When the team advanced to the NCAA Final Four in 2018, the coach who wrote this book, Porter Moser, his team, and I became a bit famous.

The Final Four win might be the reason you picked up this book. You'll learn a lot about basketball, recruitment, and strategy. You'll learn a lot more about life skills. I call Porter a "man for all seasons" because his impact on the team and students continues throughout the year as well as throughout their lives.

Having been Jesuit educated at Creighton University in Omaha, Nebraska, Porter is truly a person for others. His faith in God and his religious experience are evidenced in his personal life with his family as well as with his team. Porter encourages values based on leadership, global awareness, and service based on social justice.

These Jesuit values are part of his life as one views him at basketball practices and games; his passion for the sport; his teaching skills with the team on and off the court; his local lectures; and his dealings with coaches of the various teams at Loyola University. Porter's special ability to recruit the right young man for the right Rambler position is exceptional.

His goodness is so sincere that it captivated me immediately when he came here to coach the team. His whole healthy attitude toward sports has to do with things beyond playing on the court. Not only does he know the values of a Jesuit education, he also practices them, and they rub off on the team. They're really good kids. I think our other teams have improved, too, partly from his good influence on our Loyola spirit.

Porter is interested in each individual, helping all with any difficulties they have. He also teaches them to be generous; they share the ball. They don't care who makes the basket as long as the ball goes through the hoop. You can tell when a team does not live by that. He's taught them to be friends with one another and with him. He brings a prayerful attitude as well. We pray before each game. I have to say, sometimes my prayers aren't holy—I'm asking for a win all the time. Porter's not afraid to talk about God. One of our slogans is "Worship, Work, and Win" and we have to do all those things. Those words are up in the weight room as well, so the students see them all the time.

He's a good father, and that has a lot to do with his work with the team. When a young man makes a mistake on the court, Porter talks to him right away; there's no punitive quality to it. The young man sits down, then pretty soon, Porter puts him back on the floor. If a player does something really spectacular, Porter lets him come off the court and take a little rest, but before he sits down, he commends him. Then he goes out on the court again. Everybody sees that.

The entire student body recognizes him as a friend. After games, you hear, "Porter, Porter!" After they congratulate the opposing team, he and the team go around the whole arena and thank the Pep Band, the Spirit Teams, and the student fans for their attendance. The students wait for that—they don't even leave. They're grateful for that. So many of the students are excited about Loyola sports. The Final Four had such an effect on them—it happened before final exams. I was asking students, "How come everyone is so happy before finals?" They answered, "Sister Jean—the Final Four!"

Porter's the boss and a great man to work with. He tolerates some of the things I do. He never says, "Don't do that, Sister Jean," such as when I do my scouting report—but I know that I'm on the same page as he is. People ask me, "Sister Jean, do you pray during games?" and I say, "You better believe it!"

I hope other coaches will take this book to heart. I think a lot of other people will want to read it as well, especially if they're involved in basketball. I think high school coaches will read it. Athletes will read this—all kinds of athletes. This is easy reading, but it's deep. Porter writes it that way because it comes from his heart.

Enjoy Porter's style, his honesty, and his integrity as he describes his personal experiences as an undergraduate basketball player at Creighton University; how he overcame his sense of failure, how in his professional life perseverance, failure, adversity, passion, humility, enthusiasm, and energy played such important roles.

And, yes, the culture that he and his Final Four team of 2018 created is one to be admired. His young men learned more than basketball skills: they learned lifelong skills and are continuing to practice them and teach them to others. If you want to see a coach dedicated to his team and to his passion for basketball, just come to Chicago and attend a men's basketball game in our Gentile Arena.

INTRODUCTION: DEFINING MOMENTS

I often think of the time I had to tell my then-eight-year-old daughter Jordan that I was no longer going to be the coach of the Illinois State Redbirds. I think about the look on her face, about how her face started to crumble and her eyes teared up. I think about the pit in my stomach. Telling my family that I had been fired was the worst day of my professional life. But what I now think about most from that day is how I responded to that fact and the feeling it gave me. I wasn't going to let failure define who I was as a person. That failure led me into what I call "competitive reinvention," in which I used my energy, my positivity, and my passion to find a way to succeed.

There are a lot of different ways to define success. You can be successful when you achieve certain professional or personal goals—that might mean getting a scholarship to play basketball at a Division I school or winning a conference title. For someone else, success might mean landing that dream job right out of school. And for yet another person, success might mean having a great family and a deep faith. I've measured success in all these ways at one point or another in my life. I played Division I basketball at Creighton University, where we won the Missouri Valley Conference. I have a dream job coaching collegiate basketball at Loyola University Chicago, and our team went to the Final Four of the NCAA Tournament in 2018. I have a great family, a wonderful wife, and terrific kids. And I try to be the best man of God that I can be by living a faith-filled life that I hope gives glory to God.

But when I reflect on my successes, I can't help but recognize the hardships I had to overcome to achieve them. Success doesn't come easily. You have to be driven by something. You must have an energy about yourself that motivates you to overcome obstacles. That energy can come from a vision you have about who you—or what your future—could be. That energy can come from your faith, beliefs, or values. Whatever it is, that source of energy is what drives you to respond to adversity with positivity.

There's a word that describes that source of energy for me: *passion*. When an obstacle prevents you from obtaining something that you want, it's a gut-check moment. Will your *passion* or desire for what you want push you through whatever is standing in your way? The answer to that question can be the difference between success and failure. If your answer is "Yes, my desire is greater," you will find a way to succeed. On the other hand, if your answer is "No, not today," then success will remain out of reach. When I was fired from Illinois State, after some time spent reflecting, I still had a strong desire to coach again. It was my passion, and so I found a way. Without that desire, that *passion*, I wouldn't be coaching today, my team wouldn't have made it to the Final Four, and you wouldn't be reading this book.

When you are driven by passion and energy, you will find a purpose. I found my purpose in coaching basketball—not through wins and losses but by having an influence on the young men I coach, the student body at Loyola, and the kids who attend my basketball camps. When you have that deep sense of purpose, that personal mission, and a way to fulfill it, you will find happiness because you are satisfying your deep-seated desires. Yes, I want to be a Division I basketball coach. Yes, I want to win championships. But I also want to be a person of influence. I want to have a positive impact on the people in my life. That purpose motivates me; it directs my passion and focuses my energy. It makes me grateful for the people I've met and for the opportunities I have to make a positive difference in the lives of others.

I've learned a lot of lessons on how to be a person of influence. There are the hard lessons I've learned from responding to adversity. I've also learned about humility in facing those challenges. There are the invaluable lessons I've learned from my parents: having a strong work ethic, maintaining a positive mental attitude, and putting others first. There are the lessons I've learned from my mentors: always putting family first, finding a work-life balance, and building culture the right way. Then there are the lessons I've learned from being part of something bigger than myself. Coaching at Loyola University Chicago, I see myself as part of not just a great educational institution but of a tradition that goes back to the founding of the Society of Jesus in the sixteenth century. These lessons and others have helped me be a person for others, and they have helped me realize that what makes me happy is not how much money I make or how many championships I win but how I've had an impact on others.

Most importantly, these lessons have led me to live a life of gratitude. I see gratitude as a gift that I can give others to make them feel special and valued. When I look back at some of the worst moments of my life—such as telling my daughter that I was no longer going to be the Redbirds coach—I realize that they led me to experience some of the best moments of my life. Those hardships became defining moments for me. I would not be the person I am without them. And yeah, they sucked. But in the end, I'm grateful for all of them.

In the pages that follow, I share with you stories and lessons learned from some of my heroes, hardships, successes, and defining moments. You'll find that passion, energy, and purpose have driven me to get to where I am today: to be the best version of myself, the best coach, the best husband, the best father, and the best man of God. Maybe these stories (and the little bit of wisdom they contain) can inspire you to find passion, energy, and purpose in your own life and to become the best version of *yourself* too.

1

ENERGY AND PASSION

There's a saying I share with my players at the beginning of every season (and which I also send to my kids on our family group chat): "How you think is how you feel, how you feel is how you act, and how you act is what defines you." I believe completely in the progression of these three statements. If you're thinking good thoughts, you're going to have a bounce in your step. You're going to act in a certain way. Likewise, if you're thinking negative thoughts, if you have a "poor me" attitude, that's how people will perceive you. I make a point to maintain that positive mental attitude, something I learned from my mom, in everything I do. That's a big part of how I've found success. But I know that I couldn't have done it alone. That's why I look for players, coaches, and others who can bring that energy to what we are building. These are the people I want around me because they are the ones who will help me build our culture and bring success to our program.

Having players of high energy and character who have high values is the basis for how we have built the men's basketball program at

1

Loyola University Chicago (LUC). Yes, I want skilled players. But their outstanding skills go hand in hand with strong character. I want energized players who want to get an education, not just major in basketball. And by character, I mean belief in a value system. Some of the values I look for include respect for oneself, the team, and the culture that binds that team together. I look for integrity—doing the right thing because it's the right thing to do. I also look at a recruit's circle of influence. I don't want my players to receive mixed messages. I want to make sure that the values we espouse as part of our team culture are reinforced by the player's circle of influence, meaning the people he has around him—family, friends, mentors, and former coaches.

When I say *culture*, I mean the common values and vision that a group of people believe in. When you have a team that shares a common set of values, then you can build a culture, and that culture becomes a brand. It's what you stand for and how people perceive you. You build culture by setting expectations and standards for how you behave. We have a culture within the walls of the locker room, on the court, and on campus. You build it by holding one another accountable to the expectations and standards that are set forth by the coach, the school, and the team. This common vision is the foundation of our program. I was once asked, "What does culture mean at Loyola University Chicago?" I pointed to a picture I have on the wall in my office that had run in the *Chicago Tribune* after our Final Four run in 2018. It was a photo of me and the graduating seniors on that team and the Final Four emblem, with the caption "#1 Graduation Rate in the Country." When the whole country got to know our team, they saw what a close-knit group of high-character guys they were. The circle of positive characteristics that feeds our culture is always expanding.

Energy and positivity are an important part of who I am, and I want to surround myself with people who are positive and have high energy. The best teams are those where your best players are your leaders. It's the same for companies: your top performers set the tone. If they're not setting the right tone, it will be hard for others to follow. I look for those positive characteristics in the players I recruit to the program. But it's a two-way street: it has to be a good match for the player as well. When student-athletes are trying to decide where they are going to play in college, they need to find a way to get the attention of coaches and show them what they can do. Players use their skills and talents to get noticed. Once they get noticed, they have certain boxes they want checked off when they are deciding whether a particular school is a good fit for them. Maybe it's the quality of the facilities on campus. Maybe they want to play in a competitive conference. Maybe they want to play for a coach who has a great reputation and plays a certain style of game. Sometimes student-athletes will pick a school based on where that school is located. It's the same for me as a coach. I have certain boxes that must be checked off when I recruit student-athletes, no exceptions.

- Do they have passion and energy?
- Do they have character and respect?
- Do they want to be part of something bigger than themselves?
- Do they come from a winning program and culture?
- Do they play tough and smart?

My energy helps me in recruiting. When Clayton Custer announced he was going to transfer from Iowa State in 2015, I knew that this was a great young man who would be a perfect fit for Loyola and that Loyola was a perfect fit for him. With one day left in the recruiting period, I flew to Des Moines, rented a car, and drove to Ames to have lunch with Clayton. For the next two and a half hours, I explained why he should come to Loyola. That night I drove from Ames to Kansas City to meet his parents and talk to them. That effort paid off: Clayton committed to Loyola, where he was a huge key to our success. **Instead of saying it was too hard a trip to make, I made it happen. My energy and passion drive me. It's at the center of everything I do. It goes back to the old saying: the harder you work, the luckier you get.**

I'm looking to fill my program with people who are driven to succeed. When I hire someone, energy is at the top of the list. I ask a series of questions: What is the temperature of the room going to be when they walk in? Is it going down? Or is it going up? What's the mood going to be? I don't want the mood, or energy, to be going down. I want someone to ignite the room, to raise the mood, to bring that positive energy. I challenge my assistants and my players to bring it harder than I do at practice because they know I'm going to bring it every day. My assistant coach Drew Valentine is one of the highest-energy guys I have on staff at Loyola. That's why I hired him. When I talked to Tom Izzo, Drew's boss at Michigan State, he told me that Drew's energy level was equal to his. That's a lot of energy. And he wasn't kidding. I love coaching practice with Drew every day because he brings his energy to the floor, and he has fun. His energy is contagious. Energy is who he is. I always joke that he's a first-team All-American trash talker who gets people fired up, including myself.

If you want culture, you recruit or hire culture. Everybody who joins our program, athletes and staff included, reads *The Energy Bus* by Jon Gordon. That book outlines the way I want to build the culture of our program: create a positive vision; have a purpose; get the right people on the bus; fuel the ride with positive energy and enthusiasm; keep energy vampires off the bus; and work hard and enjoy the ride. Maintaining that culture was a big part of the Final Four run. **I've also learned from Jon Gordon that it's important to count your blessings; look at challenges as growth opportunities (we emphasize learning); talk to yourself, don't listen to yourself; feed yourself with positive encouragement; and choose faith instead of fear.** I'm constantly referencing Gordon to motivate our players, even to the point of texting quotes from his books to the team. Little acts like these send a big message: "I care." For example, I texted Lucas Williamson and Cameron Krutwig, our team captains, a quote from Gordon's book *Training Camp*: "One person in pursuit of excellence raises the standards of everyone around them. Be that one person today." These reminders set the tone for what we are doing at Loyola.

That tone is reflected on game day. I love that the guys will jump from their seats whenever we make a big play, like a blocked shot, a dunk, or a key three-pointer. Even though there's a rule that players must stay seated during the game, I want the official to come over to me and say, "Hey, Porter, get your team to sit down." I'll point to the guys on the bench and make it look like I'm telling them to sit down, but I'm actually telling them, "Great job; keep getting fired up!" Of course, if I get warned that I might get a technical foul, then I'll make sure that they do sit down. But early in the game, I'm not going to corral our enthusiasm. You can see that energy in the way I pace the sidelines during a game; I'm oblivious to it until I'm watching the tape of the game. That energy is just part of who I am and who we are as a team. At some point during the game, I know I will take off my jacket and toss it aside. When I was at Illinois State, fans would guess how long into the game it would be before I tossed my jacket aside. At Loyola, some fans started a Twitter account called @PortersJacket, which covers the game from the point of view of my discarded jacket.

I never realized that was such a big deal, but I love it—I love that people are getting a kick out of my energy. And I love that it gets them excited. My jacket stays on longer now, but I'm not sure if that's because I've matured or because we've gotten better.

Of course, there is also negative energy—energy that doesn't uplift, inspire, or radiate joy. Negative energy brings you and everyone around you down. Enthusiasm is contagious, but anyone who has been involved in team sports knows that negativity and resentment are contagious too. Negativity can spread like wildfire. You have to be on guard for negative energy in whatever form it takes: talking back to the coach, yelling at your teammates, disrespecting the officials, complaining. If I'm watching tape of a game and see guys sulking on the bench or I don't see them jump up when one of their teammates makes a big play, I see negativity. They are communicating to me—and to everyone around them—that something is off. They might be upset about something—maybe they're annoyed with their lack of playing time or pissed that they got pulled from the game. Whatever it is, their body language communicates that they don't care, and that's unacceptable. That's why we practice our body language. When the guys are tired during practice, I don't let them bend over and grab their shorts to catch their breath. That tells everyone that they are exhausted. The opposing team will pick up on that. Instead, I have them stand up and place their hands behind their head. When they come off the floor, I have them sprint because if they walk, that tells me that they are upset about leaving the game. It's okay to be upset about coming out of a game; I was a player, and there were times when I got pulled out of a game, and I didn't like it. But care enough about the team not to show your disappointment because, in the end, it's not about you—it's about the team.

Paying attention to body language is key to understanding if you're working with positive or negative energy. I pay a lot of attention to body language. A person's body language can undermine what he or she is trying to say. For example, if I'm in a conversation with another person, and I'm leaning back with crossed arms and not making eye contact, I'm communicating that I'm not interested in what that person has to say. He or she receives the message that I am disinterested. Don't let your body language send a message you don't want to send. I once had a player who would shake my hand softly and look down when greeting me. The message he was sending me was that he was not interested in meeting me—there was a lack of energy. I told him that when shaking someone's hand, look the person in the eye and smile (even if it's a half smile). That says "I'm glad to meet you" without uttering a single word. You can communicate so much by making eye contact and smiling. I remember seeing Clayton Custer put so much pressure on himself with fifteen or sixteen games left in the 2018–2019 season. He looked miserable. I said to him, "Today in practice, you have to smile at me three times. Look, you're going to be on the Mount Rushmore of Loyola basketball. Your legacy is set. Have some fun with this." I held Clayton to that. At the next game, there was a point when he came over to me after making a free throw. We both smiled—we were having fun.

There are also people who have tons of energy when everything is going their way, but when things don't go well, they're nowhere to be found. It's the guy who gets pumped after scoring two baskets in a row and sprints back on defense, shouting, "Let's go! Let's go!" But after missing three shots in a row, he's shuffling down the court, all quiet, shoulders slumped. That's another kind of negative energy.

When I coached with Rick Majerus at Saint Louis University, we used to call those guys "downhill runners." I see that a lot when I'm watching AAU (Amateur Athletic Union) games during the summer, and it cracks me up. "Where was your energy and passion during the ten minutes when you weren't doing anything?" I'll wonder. "You had no energy when you were playing defense, but you make a basket and you become 'Johnny Hype Guy.'" **I want to see a kid who misses three shots in a row sprint back on defense, clap his hands, and get his team fired up. I want to see my players have the same amount of energy when things aren't going well as they do when things are going great.**

Jon Gordon uses the term "energy vampires" to describe people who suck the energy out of the room. There are several ways to identify energy vampires. For me, I recognize their body language: they have a sourpuss look on their face, their shoulders are slumped forward, they look down as they shuffle around. These are red flags. Complaining is another indicator. "Complaining is like throwing up," Gordon writes in *The No Complaining Rule*. "Afterward you feel better but then the rest of your team gets sick." We have a team rule: "No complaining, no excuses, and no entitlement." It helps us guard against energy vampires. (I got that rule from Pete Carroll, one of only three coaches in history to win both the Super Bowl and a college national championship. He has a motto, "No complaining, no excuses." I added "no entitlement," which was something I learned from my dad.) To be honest, I don't have patience for energy vampires. To deal with them, I create an atmosphere where a negative person feels uncomfortable complaining because, if he or she does, everyone is going to call him or her out on it. I'm blunt; I call out energy vampires on their complaining as soon as I see or hear it.

But there is a difference between being an energy vampire and lacking confidence. As a coach, I think it's important to sense when a player lacks confidence. When I see that happening, I'll do what I can to lift him up. I'll show him extra film of what he's doing right and talk to him about our process. I'll share with him some of my lessons about resiliency. The key is that I address that lack of confidence right away, and I address it with something constructive like positive reinforcement and encouragement.

There is also a difference between being an energy vampire and being stressed. Sometimes we're negative because we're stressed. The key to preventing stress from turning you into an energy vampire is learning how to manage it. Being a coach for a Division I basketball program is stressful in and of itself. Fans, boosters, and the administration place expectations on you. You have a spotlight on you all the time, and when it comes down to it, success in this industry is measured by wins and losses. That's a lot of pressure. And while I'm not a perfectionist, I do have standards that I hold myself to. I am hard on myself, and in some ways, that can be a blessing. I can handle criticism from the media or from fans on Twitter because no one is harder on me than I am on myself.

Like anyone else, I get physically tired from all the travelling I do, whether it's going to games, tournaments, recruiting visits, coaches' conferences, clinics, charity outings, or speaking engagements. There are times when my basketball camps for kids, which I started a few years ago to help young people develop skills on and off the court, start the day after I've ended a long recruiting trip. I'm exhausted, and I would love to take the next day off to recover. I may think, "Damn, I have to open up camp the next day for 250 kids." But regardless of how tired I am, I have to bring it for the kids. Fortunately, I love camp, and when I get there, I get into it right away. But I am human, and I like days off as much as anyone. There are times when I've been asked to give a speech, and on the day of the event, I just don't feel up for it. I remember one time when I was asked to speak to a group of Catholic business leaders. It was after a long day of practice, and I didn't want to do it. I was tired and wanted to go home. But I had made a commitment. Sure, it would have been nice to go home, kick back, and rest in my living room in front of the TV, but I went, and I spoke for their dinner. When I got there, I switched into my speaking mode, and my energy took over. And it was great! I was able to really speak with emotion because I was speaking about my faith, how it tied into what I did, and it energized me to share it with people whose faith was important to them too.

Like any parent, I worry a lot about my kids. I love them, of course, but I also worry about how they are doing in school and in their sports. I worry when they're struggling. I also worry when I'm not physically there for them as a dad because I'm on the road for a tournament or recruiting. There's a saying that parents are only as happy as their least happy child. I carry the responsibility of fatherhood heavily. When I see that my kids are unhappy or struggling, I want to help them. But I also don't want to be a helicopter parent, and I can't solve all their problems for them. I hate seeing my children struggle, but I also want them to learn how to be resilient and fight through adversity on their own. And they can't do that if I'm always trying to fix their problems for them. It's a tricky balance. I do the best that I can, and at the very least, I let them know that I love them, even if it's in a short text message they may not have been expecting.

The truth is that sometimes I'm not great at managing stress, which means that I'm not always at my best. I need to improve on that. But there are things I do that help me. First, exercise is a big stress reliever. My coaches know that I need to get my workout in. My morning workouts help get me going and feel good about myself. They keep me energized for the day ahead. After all, I stay in shape so I can jump in during practices to demonstrate the point I'm trying to make. I feel like I'm a better coach because I'm fit. Diet goes hand in hand with exercise. I'm not a poster child for healthy eating, not by a long shot. I love what I love (and I love pizza!). But overall, I try to eat well and stay hydrated. Sticking to a balanced diet for me is a lifestyle choice, and it helps me stay healthy and energized. That's important to me. Both of my parents were heavy smokers and died at a young age, and I'm sure they would have lived longer if they had taken better care of themselves.

In addition to exercise and diet, I find ways to keep my mind active. I love to read; I'm obsessed with nonfiction during the off-season, but I switch to fiction from authors like David Baldacci and James Patterson once the season starts, just to relieve the constant stress of college basketball. I also like to end the day with my wife, Megan. I'm usually making calls until nine o'clock at night, but then Megan and I will watch our favorite shows together for an hour before going to sleep.

There's no secret to managing stress. It's about prioritizing where you focus your energy. Everybody has a lot of things going on all the time. I know I feel like I have seven or eight TVs on in my head at once, each one competing for my attention. All I can do is prioritize. I know what I need to do, and I focus on what needs to be done. Then I move on to the next thing. A lot of times I rely on other people to help keep me on task. I've also learned to listen. Listening is a practice in paying attention and being aware. You can learn so much by listening to what someone has to say and, as I explained before, by paying attention to his or her body language (as well as your own). I pay attention both to what a person says and how it's said. I value the art of listening more as I've gotten older, and I think I have gotten better at it.

Remember that saying I shared at the beginning of the book? Well, here it is again: **"How you think is how you feel, how you feel is how you act, and how you act is what defines you."** Actively listening to people, staying fit, eating right, and staying passionate and energized about what I'm doing are all part of how I live by that saying. If you maintain that approach to life, you're going to find success, some way, somehow. You can draw inspiration from other people, too. Finding those examples helps me stay motivated and energized. It's evidence that this approach to life works, and I love to share with everyone when I see those examples.

In the summer of 2019, I went to see the Rolling Stones play at Soldier Field in Chicago. I watched Mick Jagger, at age 75, jump around the stage and just kill it (and that was a few months after the guy had heart surgery). I tweeted, "Age is just a number." No one exemplifies that as much as Mick Jagger. He is the poster boy for the saying, "How you think is how feel, how you feel is how you act, and how you act defines you." If you think you're young, you'll feel young, you'll have energy, and that's how people will remember you.

I'm coaching twenty-year-old men, so I have to stay high energy. But energy isn't frenetic activity; it is focused effort, passion, and positivity. You aren't high energy because you drink a lot of coffee or do a shot of that 5-Hour Energy drink (which I have never had in my life). Being high energy has never been something that I've had to force. Energy is who I am, who I choose to be, and what I convey about myself to others. I once gave a talk to about six hundred employees of Fifth Third Bank and MB Financial Bank during their merger, and the first question during the Q & A was, "Porter, do you wear a Fitbit?" I don't, but my energy had come through in the way I was moving around on stage. That communicated that I was passionate about what I was doing, that I was prepared, and that I was going full throttle. Energy and urgency seem synonymous to me. If you approach something with energy, you'll have a sense of urgency, and you need a sense of urgency to get stuff done.

It's easy for me to have high energy because I'm lucky that I do what I love. I have energy during practice because I love teaching. I have energy during my basketball camps because I love that I have an influence on kids' lives. I have energy during games because I love being in the arena and competing. As I have gotten older, I've realized that when you have a positive, high-energy outlook, everything looks better, even when you face difficult situations. Whatever I do, I will do it with passion and energy. I am all in.

When people who know me are asked "How would you describe Coach Moser?" one of the first things they will say is that I am high energy. That's who I am, and that's the way our program is. I'm always going to fire up the crowd, even when the "crowd" is only twenty students at the game. I'll go over at the end of the game and thank them every time. Whether we play in front of dozens of fans or thousands, I am always going to get them pumped up. I want them to have the same energy that I have and that our team has. The fans are part of our culture too. Our fans fire me up. So do my players, my staff, and my family. Seeing how quick my guys are to give credit to their teammates fills me with positive energy.

And admittedly, there are days when I need that energy, passion, and commitment to keep me going, like one rainy Monday morning when I woke up congested and exhausted from a hard weekend of recruiting. I got up and worked out and then sent my kids the following text message with a picture of me after my workout:

> Today I was tired, congested, and sleepy with the rain. I didn't feel like working out. Always remember that the WANT has to be greater than how you feel. I want to be in shape, I want to be healthy, I want to be strong. So, my want was greater today. That is such a key to success, so many people stop working or grinding when they don't feel like it. Successful people's want is greater, so they push through. So, figure out what you want and have that be greater than the things that are holding you back. Love you all.

Eric Thomas, a motivational speaker and friend of the program at Loyola, taught me about your *want* having to be greater than how you feel. When you face a hardship, you can feel like crap. But your *want*—your desire to realize your vision, whatever it may be—has to be in your belly. That passion has to be there. It can make all the difference in the world between success and failure. That energy and passion will turn a hardship into your defining moment.

CREATING CULTURE

There is positive energy and negative energy. Good energy lifts you up and inspires you to share your positivity with others. That attitude can make all the difference in the world when you face adversity.

Power Up. What gives you energy? How do you stay positive?

Surround Yourself with Positivity. Who are the positive people in your life? How can they be a source of energy for you?

Exercise. How can you exercise your body, your mind, and your faith? How do these practices relieve your daily stress?

Beware of Energy Vampires. Who are the people who suck the energy out of a room? How can you prevent them from bringing you down? How can you lift them up?

2

FALL SEVEN, RISE EIGHT

Anybody can be that downhill runner, having energy when things are going great. But having energy when things don't go great, that's hard. In the summer of 2019, we celebrated the one hundredth birthday of our team chaplain, Sister Jean Dolores Schmidt. A guy from Cincinnati walked up to me with his daughter. "I have another daughter," he told me, "rowing at San Diego State, and she was about to quit." He went on to tell me that she had watched me on CBS's *NCAA Men of March*, a thirty-minute program profiling coaches from the Final Four. "She saw that you had a difficult time at Creighton," he continued, "and she felt the same way you did. She was struggling because she wasn't the star, she wasn't doing well, and she was thinking about transferring."

I said, "Get out your phone. We're sending her a video."

"Are you kidding me?"

"Why not?" I said. He started recording me, and we sent her a video of me encouraging her, telling her to not give up, **that adversity**

doesn't define us; how we respond to adversity does. Character is how you respond when things don't go your way.

I have a mantra: "Fall seven, rise eight." (It's also a line from Proverbs 24:16—"though they fall seven times, they will rise again.") I don't have a tattoo, but if I did, it would be those words. No matter how many times I might fall, I always remind myself to get up, to keep fighting, to persevere.

There's an exercise I learned from Jon Gordon that I use with my team, called "Hero, Hardship, and Defining Moment." Essentially, everyone on the team needs to share the name of a hero, a hardship he endured, and one defining moment in his life. I take part in this exercise too. When I do this exercise with them, my heroes are guys like Tony Barone, my college coach at Creighton; Rick Majerus, a legendary coach for whom I worked as an assistant at Saint Louis University; and most importantly, my parents. Naming a single hardship isn't any easier. Like most people, I've had many. That's the point of the exercise, to make you search for the examples that stand out. The one that usually comes to mind is when I got fired from Illinois State. But my defining moment was my experience as a player at Creighton University. That's where I really had to learn to live that mantra, "Fall seven, rise eight."

I was a walk-on at Creighton University after being a star player at my high school, Benet Academy, a Catholic school outside Chicago. While at Benet, we had an overall record of 70–14 and won three conference championships. I was selected to the all-conference team three times and named conference MVP my senior year. I was a star player on a good team, and that was a big part of how I thought of myself. It's easy to let your status as a sports star define who you are;

sports can become one's entire purpose in life. I was a popular kid in high school, and a lot of that was because I was good at basketball.

But as a Creighton Bluejay, that was no longer the case. I wanted to go to Creighton because there were a couple of boxes I could check off. My Catholic faith was—and still is—important to me, so I wanted to go to a school that lived that faith. Creighton is a Jesuit school. Check. Coach Tony Barone was the head coach, and he had a reputation as a tough and energetic coach who coveted the same in his players. Check. I knew that's where I wanted to play. And so, in the fall of 1986, as a freshman at Creighton University, I walked onto the basketball team. Coach Barone had seven freshmen on the team—the other six had scholarships. Even though I was a walk-on, I still expected that I'd be treated the same as the others who had scholarships. On the first day of practice, our jerseys were laid out in our lockers. Everyone had their names on their jerseys except me. Mine just had my number, #20. When I asked why my jersey didn't have my name, I was told, "You're lucky you even have a jersey." That was a reality check. Right out of the gate, I realized that I was no longer that star player I had been in high school.

My experience as a basketball player changed that day, and this became one of the toughest times in my life. Everyone who plays basketball—or any sport—at an NCAA Division I college was among the best at his or her sport in high school. The same was true for me. From the time I could bounce a ball though my senior year, I had always thought I was the best player on every team I had been on. But when I got to Creighton, I realized I wasn't. I went from being a starter and conference MVP to the eighth guard on a team of thirteen players, which means that I never played, let alone started.

It's hard to go from being the best to being irrelevant. Many athletes define themselves by their success in their sport, and I was no different. Suddenly, my identity became defined by *not* playing. Without that consistent time on the court, I wasn't sure who I was anymore. I asked myself, "Who am I if I am not playing basketball?" Basketball defined me; if I couldn't play, I felt lost. I began to wonder if the popularity I had in high school was only because I was a star on the court. If that was true, now that I wasn't playing, I began to doubt myself. I doubted my skills, my talents, even my likability. I thought about transferring. Maybe if I could play at another school, I wouldn't have those doubts.

That first year, I spent a lot of time at St. John's Church on Creighton's campus. I lived in Swanson Hall, and St. John's was within fifty yards of my dorm room. It had a candlelight student Mass at ten p.m. that I would go to every Sunday. Before every game, I would stop by St. John's to pray. That church became a refuge. I had a lot of thoughts swirling around my head about what I should do—I felt like I was being pulled in many different directions—and I needed quiet time alone to sort them out. Should I stay, or should I go? Am I not any good at what I do? Who am I? I would pray to the Holy Spirit to help guide my thoughts, give me clarity about what I should do, find the peace of mind that I would make the right decision, and I asked for the strength to follow through on whatever I decided.

I found myself at a crossroads: I could transfer to another school, or I could stay at Creighton. Transferring to another school certainly had its appeal. We hadn't quite jelled as a team yet; the freshmen were close, but we hadn't really connected with the older players, those whom Coach Barone had inherited from the previous coach. In addition, I wasn't the only one who was struggling. My roommate ended up transferring, as did three others from that first recruiting class. But then again, changing schools might not make everything better. In the end, I decided to stay at Creighton, to fight it out and persevere.

Even though I had chosen to stay at Creighton, I still had to commit myself to that decision. I had to reaffirm my choice every day. And staying didn't mean things got any easier, not by a long shot. The workouts were physically and mentally challenging. I had to rely on my energy, positivity, and passion to face the fact that I was not contributing any minutes of playing time. My focus shifted toward contributing to the team in any way I could. Staying energized and enthusiastic became part of my process, and it helped me be all in, all the time, regardless of the results. I knew that if I let up at all I'd never have a shot at playing. Second, I had to find a reason for the coaches to move me up. I was way down on the depth chart; a lot of guys would get more playing time before I would. So, I focused my time on what I could control. I chose to be positive and grateful. "Hey, I'm on this team playing college basketball," I'd tell myself over and over. My positivity eventually outweighed my negative thoughts. I knew I wasn't the most physically gifted guy on the team, and no amount of time in the gym would make me grow from 6′2″ to 6′7″. But I had a skill at shooting the ball, and I put in a lot of extra time to become elite at that skill. Finally, I took care of myself. I stayed healthy and avoided injury.

And you know what? Nothing happened. At least not at the beginning. I was going weeks without any sign of making progress. Guys were still ahead of me on the depth chart, and I still wasn't getting any playing time. But I constantly—and I mean constantly—visualized what I wanted, what my end game was. I imagined what it would be like to contribute to the team, to be counted on every game day. That *want* kept burning in my heart and trumped any self-pity and doubt I had. I remember going back to my dorm at the end of the day, exhausted from having worked my ass off, and thinking that I had not made any progress that day. That was my reality for months. Still, I kept doubling down on my decision to stay and fight, choosing to focus on my *want* and keeping a positive attitude. And that effort did bear results: at the end of my freshman year, I was given a plaque for being the Most Inspirational Player.

Looking back, I'm proud of that award! But at the time it felt like one of those trophies they give for participation. My initial reaction was to feel embarrassed. But I quickly changed my tune. I could have sulked and been resentful. Instead, I realized that even though I didn't get court time, I had contributed to the team the one thing I could: my energy. And you know what? That energy, that positive attitude—that drive—did not go unrecognized.

Halfway through my sophomore year, I was still sitting on the bench. But things were different. I had made good friends, my faith was strong, and I was still focused on the positive. The team had become more of a family under Coach Barone. Only three of Coach Barone's first recruiting class—me, Todd Eisner, and Matt Roggenburk—had chosen to stay at Creighton, and these guys had become my best friends, a friendship that continues today. I kept going to St. John's Church to pray and think things through. I kept saying to myself, "God has a plan." I had faith that at some point, there would be a breakthrough. I didn't know what that breakthrough would be or when it would come, but I trusted that God had a plan and that I would eventually figure it out.

A breakthrough finally came, though it was after a particularly bad loss. Coach Barone was completely pissed at our team for getting drilled by Notre Dame at Notre Dame. For Coach Barone, a Catholic guy from Chicago, that was unacceptable. We had a week off before our next game, which was against our conference rival Drake, followed by Marquette, another Jesuit school. Coach told us that the five guys who practiced the hardest would start the next game. I knew this was my chance. For the first year and a half of my college career, I felt that I had fought and competed with nothing to show for all that effort. I wanted an opportunity—just one chance to show what I could do, and Coach Barone had just given it to me. No one was going to practice harder than I did. And if he was telling the team the truth—and he had always told the truth, I trusted him—I knew I had a shot. And it was up to me to take it. For the next week, all we did were the kind of toughness drills you would do during the first week of practice. Charge drills, loose ball drills, corridors—nothing you'd want to do during February in the weeks leading up to the conference tournament. It was a mini-bootcamp. By the end of that week, when Coach Barone announced the starters, he said my name. I had wanted to be a contributor for so long, to influence the outcome of a game, and now I had my chance. It felt great sitting in the locker room before the game, listening to Coach Barone talk about the game plan and knowing that I was finally going to be part of that. We all wanted to contribute; that was part of the culture at Creighton.

Don't get me wrong. Even though I had worked hard and visualized this moment for two years, I had a lot of anxiety. This was my chance, and I didn't want to blow it. But I didn't let those feelings slow me down. I focused on moving forward, and I continued to work at full throttle.

I started the last few games of the season. And I did well: we beat Drake, and I scored eight or nine points; we beat Marquette, and I scored in double digits. Then we beat Southern Illinois in the first round of the Missouri Valley Conference tournament before losing to Bradley in the second round. I had achieved my goal. I had contributed to the team with playing time, and even though in the end we didn't win a title, I had proved to my coaches, my teammates, and myself that I could play hard and score. My decision to stay at Creighton, to keep a positive attitude, and to persevere had finally paid off.

The following year, the 1988–1989 season, I was a junior and had received a scholarship. That season we were picked to finish last in the Missouri Valley Conference. But we believed in our team, not the rankings. We had come together as a tight-knit family; we supported and trusted one another. It can be difficult when people from different backgrounds come together, but for me, as someone who had (and still has) a supportive family, it was important.

It was a great season. We played well together, and we had fun. Going into our last game of the regular season, we were 10–3 in the conference. After having been picked to finish last, we had a shot to be conference champions. All we had to do was beat Drake on their home court. And we did. We won 69–60. Coach Barone ripped off his shirt, revealing the T-shirt he wore underneath that said "MVC Champions." That night, on our drive back to Omaha, Coach Barone got on the radio and invited the student body to join us to cut down the basketball nets in the old gym. We arrived at Creighton at 12:30 a.m., and the entire student section was waiting for us. The students lifted us up as we cut down the nets, and we were up all night. I was standing there with Todd and Matt—my best friends since freshman year—holding the net, wearing our championship T-shirts. I thought that this was the best moment of my life.

But it got better. We went to the conference tournament and beat Indiana State, Drake (again), and Southern Illinois, becoming the MVC Tournament champs and earning a bid to the NCAA

Tournament. It was a surreal moment. I had begun my career at Creighton as a walk-on; I thought about giving up and transferring. I decided to stick it out and give it my all. I ended up becoming a starter, getting a scholarship, winning the league after being picked to finish last, and winning the MVC Tournament. And now we were playing in March Madness. I realized that if I had transferred—if I had not persevered through all the low points and disappointment—none of that would have happened. The decision to persevere had paid off, and it was the best decision I could have made.

I tell the story about my time at Creighton as an example of the power of perseverance to players who might be thinking of transferring or giving up. Maybe a player is unhappy with his lack of playing time. Maybe he's having difficulty adjusting to campus life. Maybe he's struggling with academics. Or maybe, as I did, he's fighting through one of the most difficult challenges a college athlete can face, the realization that he is no longer a high school superstar but just one high school superstar on a team of high school superstars. I tell my players who are struggling with this realization—and who think that transferring to another school will solve the problem—that the solution may not be playing on another team. A change might make everything better, but it might not. Just because they are facing adversity now does not mean that adversity isn't waiting for them somewhere else. The key to achieving success is to figure out your true desire and then come up with a vision of how to pursue it. In my case, that meant envisioning myself as a contributor to the team and being a part of a winning culture with a close group of guys.

That's the kind of culture I want to coach. The culture of our locker room at Loyola University Chicago (LUC) is built on perseverance. To keep our commitment to building this culture, I dedicated an entire wall in our locker room to slogans and phrases that remind us of the standards it is built on. One of the many sayings on our Wall of Culture is "Never Quit on a Play." Our starting guard Ben Richardson didn't give up on a play in our game against the University of Miami in the first round of the 2018 NCAA Tournament. We were down seven points, Miami was on a 7–0 run, and the game was in danger of getting away from us. Ben, one of the team leaders on and off the court, was running down the court; he stepped on the official's foot and went down, clutching his ankle, spraining it. Miami got the ball. Ben then got up, ran back into the play, stole the ball from the Miami player, and passed to an open Marques Townes, who drove in for a layup. It was a complete momentum changer. When I look at that game, I think about that play a lot. Ben had sprained his ankle, and instead of staying down or yelling at the official for tripping him, he didn't stop. Only when a timeout was called afterward did Ben limp off the court. That's what never quitting on a play looks like.

Every day we start practice by watching clips from the previous practice or the previous game. We film practice so that we can review video together. I call out examples of perseverance so that the guys know what it looks like. We'll pull out ten to fifteen clips of things we have to do better, ten to fifteen clips that emphasize different phrases on our Wall of Culture. I show clips from games where we played with perseverance and tenacity. I call our film sessions "Get Better Tapes." This changes the mindset—some people might have the mindset of watching film as an ass-ripping session, and they dread it. We look at film differently. It's an opportunity to improve. We start with pointing out what can be done better, but I also point out the intangible characteristics that make up our culture, the values we want to promote as a team and the ones that elevate our game. We look at perseverance as a separator between us and the competition.

No team is going to have a smooth road to the championship. All teams are going to face adversity: bad calls by the refs, injuries, shots that go in and out. Everyone faces adversity of some kind. You can't hide from it. The choice we make over and over again is how to respond to it. **I always share with my players my definition of character: "Character is how you respond when things don't go your way."** I already offered you this definition at the beginning of this chapter, but it's important. Whatever you are going through, there are several ways you could respond. One of the most important is for you to find a sanctuary, a place where you can be alone to think. There's so much noise and busyness in life. Having a refuge as I did at St. John's Church at Creighton creates the space to separate you from the noise and make room for clarity. When you talk to yourself, ignore the negative thoughts that try to fill you with doubt. Instead, visualize your desire and articulate it; let that vision motivate you. Feed on it. You must have a *want,* and that *want* silences the voice that is telling you to quit. You also acknowledge that it's not going to be easy sailing. If overcoming adversity were easy, there would never be adversity. But adversity gives us the opportunity to shape who we are by responding with perseverance.

You make choices about how to overcome adversity, and those decisions lead to defining moments, the key times in our lives when we discover who we really are. My decision to stay at Creighton is MY defining moment. I've gone back to that moment many times over the past 35 years. If I had thrown in the towel at Creighton, I wouldn't be coaching. I wouldn't have met my wife. I wouldn't be impacting people. I wouldn't have the friendships I've made along the way. But I didn't quit. I went to the NCAA Tournament. I became a coach. I have made a great living doing something that I love. If I had given up because it was a little hard, none of these things would have happened.

A final note: Perseverance is more than "toughing it out." It means not letting adversity define who you are in a negative way. It means seeing clearly the challenges that you are facing, understanding what your values are, and responding to those challenges in a way that is true to those values. Some of the greatest moments of my life happened to me after some of the worst times in my life or when things didn't go my way. Perseverance forces you to think, to find the ways to succeed when things get tough. Perseverance is a level of strength and tenacity that cannot be found in the weight room or on the basketball court; it's found through discernment and introspection. Perseverance is where the real victories are found; it's in getting up the eighth time after having fallen a seventh.

CREATING CULTURE

We all face adversity in a variety of forms. How we respond to adversity can become our defining moments, moments that help us understand who we are, what we value, and where we fit into the world.

Stay positive. How can you keep a positive mental attitude? What is your source of energy?

Have a vision. What do you imagine for yourself? What do you desire? What is your *want*?

Find a sanctuary. Where can you go to be alone with yourself, your thoughts, and God?

Find your strengths. What are you good at? How can you excel at that skill?

3

LESSONS ON HUMILITY
AND THAT DAMN TICKER ON ESPN

There is no easy way to learn humility; to learn life's lessons, you have to live, and life will include its share of ups and downs. As I mentioned in the last chapter, in order to get up an eighth time after falling seven, you first have to have fallen seven times. No matter how many times you have to get back up, you still do. That's the "rise eight" part.

So, let's talk a little about failure. As I had mentioned earlier, the biggest failure in my professional career—my biggest fall, you could say—was when I was fired as the head basketball coach at Illinois State in the spring of 2007. That was one of the worst days of my professional and personal life.

Up until that point, I had been a successful head coach. My first head coaching job was at the University of Arkansas Little Rock in the 2000–2001 season. We won eighteen games that season, fourteen more than the previous year. It was the biggest turnaround in the history of the Sun Belt Conference. Some people would jokingly refer to UALR as "University of Arkansas, Last Resort." Sure, they were kidding, but the players heard that, and it created a negative mindset and culture. I never wanted to hear that joke again. To make sure, we immediately began to infuse energy and positivity into the program. I began signing student-athletes who reflected those values. That alone changed the culture in the UALR locker room. We were no longer a last resort; we were a destination for a certain kind of basketball player. I attribute a lot of our turnaround to that change in mindset. We recruited student-athletes who believed in UALR as a place where we could win. As a coach—or manager, business owner, or teacher, for that matter—you must have a vision of what your program is going to be like. Everywhere I've coached, I've created a vision statement of what I want for the team. At UALR that meant a team with heart, with players who valued academics and worked hard. That led me to recruit student-athletes who believed in that vision, which helped us make history in the Sun Belt Conference.

When we won eighteen games in each of the next two years, I started getting recognized as one of the top young, up-and-coming head coaches in the country. In the spring of 2004, I got a call from the athletic director of Illinois State University. He was looking for a new head coach and was interviewing people during the National Association of Basketball Coaches (NABC) conference that was held during the Final Four. He asked if I would like to meet with him and a rep from their search committee. I met with them for a few hours and again the next day. That night I was offered the head coaching job.

Illinois State offered me a six-year contract; I asked for seven because I needed time to turn the program around (plus, I had job security at UALR—I was coming off three eighteen-win seasons), and they gave it to me. Illinois State was in last place in their conference, and they had no scholarships available. I wasn't going to be able to recruit the guys I wanted until my second year at the earliest. I had a culture in mind that I believed in: a high-energy environment with guys who don't quit and who prioritize academics. It was going to take time to build that culture. Plus, the Missouri Valley Conference had strong teams. Creighton, Wichita State, Southern Illinois, Northern Iowa, Bradley, and Missouri State were all loaded with talent. You were not going to go from last place to the top overnight.

UALR countered with a ten-year contract, and, once again, I found myself at a crossroads. I loved coaching at UALR, and I had a talented team coming back. But coaching at Illinois State would give me the opportunity to coach in the Missouri Valley Conference, the conference where I had played and won a conference championship at Creighton. It was the state school of my home state, and I would be closer to family and friends. Plus, I saw an opportunity to repeat what I had done at Little Rock: to be a person of influence, to take over a last-place program, build an environment with high-character student-athletes, and turn around a struggling program. I took the job.

I knew the job at Illinois State wasn't going to be easy. We continued to struggle at first, winning only ten games during my first season as head coach, marginally better than the year before. But I had a process. I recruited talented guys who showed respect for themselves, others, and the program, young men who wanted to be part of something bigger than themselves and who played tough and smart. I focused on developing a strong defense. We were much improved our second year, winning seventeen games and placing sixth in the MVC. By the 2006–2007 season, we had improved significantly, and with only one senior among our top nine players, I was going to get my entire team back for 2007–2008. We were loaded with talent: one of our returning players, Osiris Eldridge, had been named the MVC freshman of the year. Illinois State was picked to win the MVC in 2007–2008. We were poised to make a great run. I was excited and confident.

That's when my world was rocked. Illinois State was going through a lot of changes at the time. I had three different athletic directors in four years. That meant three different bosses, each with different ideas and priorities. Then, my last athletic director bought out the last three years of my contract. In short, I had been fired. It was a punch in the gut. Here I was, an up-and-coming coach who had proved himself at Little Rock and was making progress the right way at Illinois State. Our talent was improving. We were scrupulous in complying with NCAA rules. The team average GPA went from 1.9 to 2.9, and we had no problems within the community, on campus or off. So when the rug was pulled out from under me, I was crushed. I had put in four years of my life, blood, sweat, and tears to get the right young men, build a culture, and turn the program into a winning, admirable, hard-working team. I felt that our team at Illinois State was ready to win, and then in a single moment, I was no longer going to be part of it.

Being fired as a head coach of a Division I college basketball program makes the news. You're subjected to a level of shame and scrutiny that doesn't exist with other jobs, unless you're the CEO of a huge corporation. On that long, disappointing day, you could have walked into any sports bar or restaurant in the country and watched the ticker on the TV scroll "Porter Moser fired from Illinois State." In my mind, nothing could have screamed *FAILURE!* more clearly than the damn ticker on ESPN. I wondered if that's how people would see me: the guy who failed at Illinois State. For someone who is a competitor like me, the idea that people might see me as less than a success killed me. I felt as if someone had a foot on my neck. Then, after the humiliation, the fear set in. I started to worry about my family. How was I going to support them? What was I going to do next? It was emotionally exhausting.

The next morning, when I got up and looked at the front page of the local paper, *The Pantagraph,* I saw it again: "Redbirds Fire Moser." I couldn't control ESPN or the local newspaper, so I focused on what I could control: I got out of town for the weekend. My wife, Megan, and I took the family to a water park in the Wisconsin Dells. I wanted to clear my head, and I didn't want my kids to worry about what was going to happen next. Megan and I sat poolside as the kids had fun in the pool, unaware of what was going on with their dad.

"It's going to be fine," Megan reassured me. "We're going to make this work."

As I watched the kids splash and play, I realized how lucky we were. I had a great marriage, and we had four healthy kids. Megan was right. I knew everything was going to be okay. It was impossible to feel sorry for myself when I thought of my family. I was truly blessed.

Some of my coaching friends called to pump me up. "You haven't been in the profession long enough if you haven't been fired," I remember one of them telling me. Tom Crean, the head coach at Marquette University at the time, reached out to me. He was preparing his team to play in the NCAA Tournament, and he invited me to come up and sit in on all the team meetings and travel with the team. I flew to Milwaukee for a few days before we traveled to Winston-Salem to play Michigan State in the regional. I remember coming back from that experience, thinking, "I know I still want to do this. *I'm gonna do this.*" That clarity, that reminder of my life's passion, was another blessing.

Now, I can't sit here and say that I was suddenly telling myself, "Hey, I'm strong. I'm going to get through this," because it's not true. I didn't feel strong. I felt weak. I was devastated. I was suffering a very real sense of loss. Even if you are a person of faith—I knew God had a plan and I always trusted in that plan—it's hard to say "Oh, it's okay" and let it slide. I was bitter and angry. I prayed not to feel that way, and I still felt that way for a long time. "God has a plan," I kept repeating to myself. I realized that whatever God's plan was, it did not include feelings of bitterness, resentment, and anger.

As I look back on that time, I realize that there were indeed blessings hidden in that failure. First and foremost, I had my family. They were the most important people in my life; nothing could ever change that. Second, I learned that I could lean on the people who really cared about me. When Tom Crean reached out to me to join Marquette for their NCAA run, I knew that there were people in the profession who would help me rebound from this loss. And finally, I recommitted myself to coaching. I was not going to let this failure define me and end my career.

It's easy to be on the top of the world when you're winning games and conference championships, playing in postseason tournaments, and going to the Final Four. But it's the losses that teach you the best lessons. So many people want to blame everyone and everything else for their failures. But I've learned that the blame game doesn't make you better. You can't learn why you didn't play your best if you're blaming the referee. Competitors want to know *why* they lost so they can improve. After a bad loss, we'll look at the tape and ask "Why?" a lot. *Why didn't we play our best? Why didn't we perform? Why didn't we execute?* When you win, you might not dig as deep into those questions as you do when you lose. But you need that mindset. That's how you make corrections and improve your ability to play the game. It's in the experience of the defeats when you learn the true meaning of humility: you see what you need to improve. **The real measure of success is how you emerge from defeat, from adversity, from rugs being pulled out from under you.** I want to teach the young men on my team that when the losses come—and they will, it's college basketball, after all—no matter how bitter they may feel, no matter how much it stings to lose, we will use that loss to improve, to become better basketball players and better people.

Having a vision helps you bounce back from failure. At the beginning of the 2018 season, at the conclusion of our boot camp in September, the players showed up in the locker room for their last scheduled workout. They were met by the team manager, who handed them a letter that said, "You have 15 minutes to find the coaching staff on campus," and it provided a clue. That led them on a scavenger hunt, leading them to the weight room, our arena, and other places around campus. The last stop was in the Damen Student Center movie theater. They walked in, and the coaching staff was there. I brought the team to the front row and showed them a montage of teams celebrating Selection Sunday from the year before. We watched all the teams jump and cheer when they learned whom they were going to play in the NCAA Tournament. That was our vision statement for the year. That was what we wanted. Everybody wants to get to that point—whether it's being selected for March Madness or achieving another important goal. But not everyone wants to invest in the process that it takes to get there. We had just finished boot camp and were about to start the next phase of our process, which is five or six weeks of practicing without a game. That's a tough part of the year, because the games naturally serve as motivators you work toward. But six weeks is a long time. Still, that vision of what could be helped motivate us during that phase. Going through that "shared shittiness" helps build a brotherhood because you get closer as a team while going through adversity. (I guess you can say that "shared shittiness" is part of our culture, too.)

You don't need to play college basketball to understand this lesson. Failure is part of life, whether it's sports, academics, or the business world. There are times when you'll bomb a test or fail to meet a sales quota. The initial response might be disappointment, fear, and even panic—"I'm going to flunk out of school!" or "I'm going to get fired!" Those feelings will come, and they are normal. The key to living through failure is to look at that failure as an opportunity to learn how to improve. For example, if you failed a test, consider the reasons why. Was there something you didn't understand? What could you do to understand that concept better? Solutions will present themselves: maybe you'll seek out a study group to hold yourself accountable; maybe you'll reach out to the professor for extra help. The blessings that come from that failure might be new friends, better study habits, or discovering a mentor. In business, you might find that a project was an utter failure. What lessons can you learn from that failure? Did the product fail to meet the customers' needs and expectations? Was there not enough quality assurance built into the process? Was there too little (or too much) oversight? Lessons-learned meetings, or postmortems (meeting after the conclusion of a project and looking at what went right and what went wrong), can be a blessing if they help discover better ways of evaluating what customers want and need, develop processes that assure quality, and establish a more effective management structure.

Nobody wants to fail—that's a given. The key is to learn from your failures. When you build a culture that values humility, you create opportunities to learn and to grow. You come to understand that as painful as failure can be, it can lead to positive results. It takes strong character and courage to bounce back from personal defeats and find blessings when things go bad. That's the kind of character that you would want in any player on any team.

Humility is a way of life. When you live with humility, you live knowing that it's not all about you. Life is about "we"; it's about others. Humility means you're not afraid to admit your faults, and that's not a weakness. It's a positive—because you are aware of what you need to work on, to grow and to improve. Living with humility means admitting the truth that "Hey, I'm not perfect." Acknowledging a mistake is a powerful act of leadership because you humanize yourself. **When you're humble—when you admit your mistakes—you build trust. You show that, in the end, you're concerned with something beyond your own accomplishments or achievements.**

When you blame others, you're not practicing humility. Humility means that you hold yourself accountable; if you are constantly blaming others for your failures, you're not accepting responsibility for the things you might have done that contributed to that failure. Some people can't hold themselves accountable because they can't admit that they were wrong. I know this firsthand. When I was fired from Illinois State, at first I was bitter, and I blamed the athletic director. But I quickly showed restraint. All I said publicly was that I was disappointed that I didn't get a chance to finish what I started. In the years that followed, I did a lot of introspection, asking myself what I could have done differently. Successful people, especially when they feel they were wronged, take the time to reflect on what they could have done better.

Humility is not only a way to respond to failure, it's also a way to respond to success. The 2018 Final Four run was incredibly humbling for me. It was the biggest stage I could have imagined. I was getting hundreds of texts during those games. I was on *Golic and Wingo* on ESPN, and within ten minutes of that, I'm getting calls to be on *The Dan Patrick Show* and *The Jim Rome Show*. I was everywhere. But I wasn't going to make it about me; it was about the guys, it was about Loyola. The media exposure was so over the top that it would have been easy to let the fame go to my head. But that's not how I was brought up and that's not who I want to be. My mom always warned me against bragging, and that helped me understand what humility looked like. When I got to the Final Four, it would have been unnatural for me not to make it about others.

When I do public speaking or talk to my team, I bring up my time at Illinois State. I've had failures in my life, and humility allows me to look at those as opportunities to get better, to improve, to grow. And as I've had success, humility allows me to remain grateful and give credit to all the people who made my success possible, because I certainly didn't do it on my own.

In his book *Why the Best Are the Best*, Kevin Eastman, a former NBA championship coach, writes, "It's often been said that true humility is not thinking less of yourself, it's thinking of yourself less. . . . Humility keeps us on the path of self-improvement that all greats travel." **Humility says that I don't know it all. I need to learn more. I am open and available to be taught.**

Sometimes I'll ask a student athlete I'm recruiting, "What are you looking for in a program?" Too many times I've heard the response, "I want to go somewhere where I can play my game and do my thing." I cringe whenever I hear that. *Do your thing?!?* What I hear is that the athlete is all about himself. He might as well say, "It's about me." I want to say, **"You know what our thing is? Winning together."** Or I'll have recruits tell me, "I want to go to a place where I can score twenty points per game." I'll tell them, "Well, I had student-athletes who went to the Final Four and signed pro contracts averaging only eleven points per game." The answer I love to hear is "I want to be on a winning team. I want to have a family atmosphere. I want to have a close-knit group. I want to get a great education." Those are the "wants" that you can build a culture on.

A common way to think about success is achieving the goals one sets for oneself, but I'm not sure that's entirely right. Humility is key to success because sometimes failure is necessary. You find success in rebounding: to rebound a missed shot, you put yourself in position to make a play. The little blessings that you discover when you fail lead to gratitude and positivity, which will hopefully lead to long-term happiness, and happiness is the greatest success of all. Humility helps you see how failures can point you toward new opportunities that help you discover the person God wants you to be. However, that doesn't make failure easy. Nobody wants to fail, least of all me. I hate failure: it's painful, gut-wrenching, and crushing. But to find blessings within it, you need humility. You cannot see failure as an end; you must see it as an opportunity to learn how to bounce back.

CREATING CULTURE

Humility is a way of life. It is not only the way you respond to adversity but the way you respond to success. Humility requires that you look at yourself, the world, and others honestly and truthfully.

Find your values. What things are important to you, the things that can't be taken away?

Lean on others. To whom can you turn when you have faced a defeat? Who respectfully keeps you from getting too full of yourself?

Find the lesson. What does this failure teach you about yourself?

Adjust your approach. What can you do differently in the future that will help you act with humility when you're tempted to be rude in the face of defeat or boastful in the face of success?

4

COMPETITIVE REINVENTION

The reality of coaching college basketball is that you need to win to have job security. But as the saying goes, winning isn't everything. I mean that. There are a lot of good coaches who don't win. What is important to me is that we win the right way. I want to go home at night, look my kids in the eye, and say to them, "I did things the right way." It starts with the people in the locker room, the people you share the journey with. I want to share the journey with people I love. I don't want to sell my soul to get supertalented players who are interested only in getting a degree in basketball and don't fit our culture.

I recruit student-athletes who are looking to be part of something bigger than themselves. I tell recruits, "When you come to Loyola, it's more than a four-year commitment to Loyola; it's a lifelong relationship." I want us to see one another as more than just teammates, as a family, as people to be trusted and relied upon through thick and thin. And one of the values that brings our team together as a family is resiliency.

When I tell my story of getting fired from Illinois State, I could leave it at that, another story about a guy who got fired. But that simple version isn't the complete story. When I add the part about how I responded to the setback with energy, positivity, and integrity, it becomes a more nuanced and accurate story of resiliency. Resiliency is different from perseverance. Perseverance is continued effort in the face of difficulty. Resiliency is seeing the problem and adjusting to the difficulty. **Perseverance is strength; resiliency is strategy.**

To learn from failure, you need resiliency. You discover what adjustments you need to make so that when faced with a similar situation in the future, you are in a better position to avoid failing. My approach to resiliency is "competitive reinvention." The "competitive" part comes from the instinct all athletes have to push themselves to win. The "reinvention" part refers to the idea that we can choose the parts of our stories that we emphasize, the parts that help us become the person we want to be. When I got fired from Illinois State, I had to reframe how I saw myself. I didn't want the story to end that way. I decided I was going to compete to find a different ending, one that didn't end with failure. I was going to move beyond the story of "fired coach."

We all reinvent ourselves from time to time. Incoming college freshmen reinvent themselves as college students. They reinvent themselves again when they graduate. When we get married, we reinvent ourselves into one half of a committed couple. Every time we switch jobs, there is yet another opportunity for reinvention. "Reinvention" doesn't mean we change who we are; that's not what I'm saying. Rather, "reinvention" is how we reframe the stories we tell about ourselves so we can take on our adversities and draw out the best parts of ourselves.

Competitive reinvention begins with a vision: You have to know what you want to become, and you have to know that you will have to learn in order to grow into that person. For me, I wanted to be a successful basketball coach, and I needed to get to a place where I could become one. Just as I had a vision of what I wanted to be when I was a struggling player at Creighton, I had a vision of what I wanted as a coach: to be at a school where I had a purpose, where I loved the culture, and where we were winning through hard work and dedication to improving our game.

I did not want to give up that vision, but I had to face reality after the Illinois State firing. I had reached a roadblock in my career, one that I would need to get over to get back to coaching. I knew I needed to reinvent myself so that I could achieve that original vision. But that meant hard work, and I wasn't quite ready for it yet. I needed to regroup. After Illinois State, I wallowed in my sorrow for about a week, but then I launched into my competitive reinvention process. The people who know me have always known my competitiveness. I love to win, but I hate to lose more. I don't want to fail. I'm not afraid of failure. It just sucks. Growing up, my family always played sports in our backyard. Everyone in our neighborhood would get together and play whatever sport was in season: baseball, football, or basketball. Being the youngest, I wanted to show them that I had the skills to keep up with them. My competitiveness continued inside the house. My sister, Kate, and my two brothers Matt and Mitch and I would play games like Monopoly, Clue, and Michigan rummy. Whatever the game, I hated to lose. The backyard and board games fueled a competitive spirit in me that motivated me to push myself to excel at whatever I was doing. At every level of every sport I played, I was driven to win a championship because I hated losing.

When you fail, you feel that people look at you differently. I felt that people didn't want to be around me. The National Association of Basketball Coaches (NABC) has their annual convention at the Final Four, and every basketball coach in the country—coaches from NCAA Division I, II, and III schools, the National Association of Intercollegiate Athletics (NAIA) schools, junior colleges, and high schools—gathers to network with their peers. When I went to the convention after getting fired, I felt like a leper. Every time I walked into the hotel that served as the conference headquarters, I was hit with the feeling that my peers were looking at me and thinking, "Here comes the dude who just got fired from Illinois State." When you network with people, you want to show them that you have something to offer and that you will add value to their program. But as a recently fired head coach with no job, part of me was worried that people wouldn't give me the time of day. They'd look at me, say to themselves, "He can't help me," and move on. I felt toxic. As you might imagine, that feeling makes everything, even trying to network, hard. I didn't want people to think that I was defeated; I had to bring out a different part of my story.

I went to the Kingwood Classic in Houston, one of the premier AAU basketball tournaments in the country. A lot of coaches and players would be there, and I would be able to show coaches that I was up and grinding again. **If the saying "out of sight, out of mind" is true, then so is the saying "In sight, in mind."** I met student-athletes, talked to them, and evaluated their talent when other coaches couldn't: college coaches aren't allowed to watch the players on the first day of the tournament. Since I was out of a job, that rule didn't apply to me. I got a one-day head start over every other college coach at the tournament to watch, evaluate, make contacts, and build relationships with players and their coaches. That one-day advantage gave me leverage. Now I had value to bring to the table. I could tell other college coaches, "Hey, this kid can play" or "That kid would be a great fit for your program." I could show them that I could evaluate talent and build relationships, which is essential in recruiting good players.

As I mentioned before, **I believe that the harder you work, the luckier you get.** And I was working hard that day, a value I learned from my dad—but I'll get to that later. I was taking notes on the kids that I liked, meeting people, and talking to coaches. I was grinding, and I made an impression. While I was there, I managed to land an interview with the athletic director of a Division I school in Texas whose program was struggling. After the interview, the athletic director told me that they were going to fly me out the following weekend to visit the campus and meet the president of the school. At that point, I had a good feeling that I was going to get the job.

The day after that initial interview, which was a Sunday, I got a phone call from Rick Majerus. At first, I thought one of my friends was playing a joke on me. But he had such a distinctive Wisconsin accent (when he said "offense," it sounded like "OH-fence"), and after a minute, I knew my friends couldn't have pulled it off. It really was Rick Majerus on the other end of the line. He had been looking for someone with head coaching experience who could recruit in the Midwest. Three different people gave him my name as the first person he should call. We talked for two hours. Rick told me he was thinking of taking the job as the head basketball coach at Saint Louis University. He had been out of coaching for four or five years, having worked as a commentator for ESPN. We continued to talk for the next few days, and by the middle of the week he asked me whether I would go with him to St. Louis if he took the job.

I had to make a decision: Do I continue to pursue the head coaching job in Texas, which was pretty much a sure thing, or do I follow Rick Majerus—one of the greatest basketball minds on the planet—to St. Louis as an assistant coach? Rick was still negotiating the final terms of his contract. All week I was debating with myself whether to go to St. Louis or Texas.

My ego wanted me to take the head coaching job in Texas. After all, there is a lot of prestige in being a head basketball coach at a Division I school. If I joined Rick's staff at Saint Louis University (SLU), people might see it as a demotion. My ego didn't like that I had to take a step backward in my career. But my mom taught me to always have a positive mental attitude—"Porter, PMA," she used to say—and so I approached being an assistant under Rick with the same energy and positivity I had as a head coach. Instead of being disappointed, I would look at the job with Rick as an opportunity to learn from a basketball genius; it would be like getting a PhD in basketball. I was thirty-seven years old at the time, and I had a chance to reinvent myself by learning from one of the best in the business. That attitude would allow me to approach the position with passion and give 100 percent of my effort to being Rick's assistant. He was excellent in all the areas that I wanted to learn more about: the motion offense, man-to-man defense, and skill development. Everybody warned me how hard it would be as an assistant coach under Rick. He had a reputation of working his assistants to the bone, but that was never a deterrent. My want was greater than my fear—I wanted to learn as much as I could from him, and working hard was never an issue with me.

By the end of the week, Rick had taken the job at SLU, I cancelled the trip to Texas, and I started with him on day one of his tenure there.

When you face failure, you have to bounce back. You have to get competitive; you have to find the energy to get out there, talk to people, go to clinics or workshops or job fairs, learn more, and make connections. You can't sit on your couch, watching TV, waiting for the phone to ring. You have to show people that you are passionate, a grinder, and good at what you do. Hardworking people get fired in any profession, not just coaching. There can be cutbacks or new leadership with a different vision, as was my case at Illinois State. I used my firing as an opportunity to reinvent myself as a better coach by learning from a master, and that involved becoming an assistant coach under Rick Majerus. It proved to be a bigger step forward than I realized.

I was living the phrase, **"How you think is how you feel, how you feel is how you act, and how you act is what defines you"** before I ever learned it or could articulate it. Resiliency starts with your frame of mind and what truth about yourself you want to tell. My outlook has always been positive, and that is the story I chose to live. I inherited my PMA—positive mental attitude—from my mom. As I mentioned before, she would always remind me, "Porter, PMA," whenever she wanted to bolster me with enthusiasm, energy, and perseverance. I still hear those words when things get hard.

That positive attitude changed the way I felt about my coaching career at that moment. Excited about the future, I was going to use this opportunity to show everyone that I still had what it takes to succeed as a Division I college basketball coach. My job as Rick's assistant led me to the head coaching position at Loyola University Chicago, which allowed me the chance to lead them to the Final Four. **That energy and passion to remain a competitor and reinvent what it takes to grow define me.** During our Final Four run, whenever my players were asked, "How would you describe Coach Moser?" they all started with "high energy." It's who I am. And I hope my energy and passion pump people up when they face hardships, when they question their own sense of self-worth. I want them to know that they are not defined by their failures but by their resiliency.

Whenever I hear of coaches who get fired, I call them up as soon as I can to share my experience because I want to encourage them to be resilient. I'll never forget how much it meant to me that Tom Crean reached out after I was fired from Illinois State, and I want to pay it forward. I tell these guys about competitive reinvention, that they'll bounce back, that things get better. I say, "Hey, man, I think you're a great coach, and I know how things happen. You can't let this define you." I tell them that it's okay to grieve the old job, the loss of potential plans—it's necessary and healthy. I also tell them that getting back on their feet is not going to happen overnight. It will take hard work, enthusiasm, and a positive mental attitude. I want them to know that they are not alone. I don't want them to feel like they are toxic the next time they go to the NABC convention like I did. That is a horrible feeling. No one should have to go through that alone.

When my friend Mark Fox was fired as the head coach at the University of Georgia, I called him. Knowing what he was going through, I wanted to pump him up. I mentioned competitive reinvention and told him about my experience being fired at Illinois State. I shared with him how I made a choice not to let that barrier define me. I made my own breaks and found the best situation for me to reinvent myself as a coach. Mark called me after he got a new job as the head coach at UC Berkeley. He told me how the concept of competitive reinvention made him see a clearer picture of what he should do after his firing. Mark got proactive by watching other colleges practice, meeting with people from the NBA, and reaching out to search firms. Competitive reinvention really resonated with him and helped him respond to his own loss positively.

There is so much pressure today to get results quickly, not just in basketball but in the business world and in life. In basketball, the expectation might be to go from a four-win season to a twenty-win season in a single year. In the business world, CEOs feel pressure to meet the expectations of Wall Street or boards of directors. In academics, the expectation is to ace the next test, to get the best grades, to be at the top of the class. But when you fail to get the results that you and others expect, you might skip the hard work of discovering a better way to achieve them. A lack of resiliency can lead people to wallow (as I did for a week), or to find a shortcut around the hard work of self-improvement. Coaches might be tempted to violate a recruiting rule. CEOs might be willing to lie on their earnings reports to mislead investors. Students might be willing to cheat to get that A. **Resiliency, however, is seeing past the easy way out to come up with a strategy to overcome adversity and doing the hard work—grinding it out—to get the result you want.**

When I got the job at LUC, the team had had four winning seasons in the past twenty years, and they hadn't won a conference championship in thirty years. **Rick Majerus wrote me a letter, telling me, "Porter, I know you want to win right away. Build it slowly. Build the program the right way."**

I focused on recruiting student-athletes from winning programs, athletes who were good students and had high character. I made academics a priority. The process was slow, but it worked. Loyola finished first in the MVC in 2018 and 2019 and was the MVC Tournament champion in 2018, going on to win the NCAA South Region to go to the Final Four. We achieved success by building culture first and not cutting corners.

What does "the right way" to build a team look like? It means building a team that is resilient, a team that knows how to grow and learn from failures, a team that trusts in its ability to improve when confronted with challenges or setbacks. You can talk about resiliency, but when you can bring up examples to show people what it looks like, that's when it hits home. I love bringing up resiliency during teaching moments. In 2019, we lost to Southern Illinois on the road. We didn't play well, and it put us behind the eight ball in the conference. Our next two games were against Northern Iowa there and then Bradley at home. Northern Iowa and Bradley were two of the hottest teams in our league, and we had to win both games to win the conference. We talked about being resilient. It would have been easy to talk about the uphill climb we faced; we could have been resigned to the fact that we weren't going to get it done this year. But I reminded the team: "Fall seven, rise eight." It became our mantra as we prepared for Northern Iowa. It was a grinder of a game. They had a chance to win the league, and the game was on their Senior Night—everyone in the stands wore black, and they asked us to wear our home uniforms. We were playing a high-stakes game in a high-stakes environment, and we had to do it coming off a bad loss. Throughout the game, it looked like Northern Iowa was going to run away with it; at one point they scored four three-pointers in a row. But we were resilient and kept bouncing back. We won by one point, 56–55.

One of my favorite sayings is "To create culture, hire culture." I hire assistants who share my values and energy. And I am obsessed with coaching them up, with making them better at what they do. I understand the impact my assistants have on building team culture, and if my assistants understand my vision, they will be able to better share it with the players. If I am constantly helping my assistants get better, they will be able to help the players get better. Helping the people around you improve their skills is an important aspect of leadership—for themselves, for the team, for the organization. What makes a culture resilient is the commitment of people at all levels in supporting each other to be better at what they do.

Of course, there are always examples of what happens when standards are lowered or ignored. Case in point: in the fall of 2017, the FBI revealed a conspiracy between schools and athletic shoe companies. There was a large scandal that was a black mark on our profession. That's what happens when you sacrifice integrity to cut corners. I read in an article that college presidents were losing sleep over the scandal, worrying if one of their coaches was caught up in it. I immediately sent an e-mail to Dr. Jo Ann Rooney, the president of Loyola University Chicago. "Dr. Rooney," I wrote, "I just want you to know that you can fluff your pillow. You've got nothing to worry about." We had built the culture at Loyola the right way.

Resiliency is an essential characteristic of a good culture. I know that I will face future setbacks; being a college basketball coach is a difficult profession, not known for its job security. When we failed to make the NCAA Tournament in 2019, I was pissed. We had been to the Final Four the year before, and our entire process was directed toward getting us back to the tournament. But we turned that disappointment into a positive: we got a bid to the National Invitation Tournament (NIT). Only thirty-two teams get a bid to the

NIT—Loyola hadn't been in nearly forty years—and we were one of them. I was proud of our guys for how they reacted to the incredible pressure they faced every day after the Final Four run. I was proud of their resiliency in winning another league championship.

Your life's journey has big losses and small ones. You can have a great record and win championships, but a loss against a rival during the regular season can sting the most. I can have a great recruiting class but losing one guy to another school hurts. But, adversity is just another name for opportunity. Every time we lose a game, even if we're having a great year, we can use that loss to get stronger, smarter, and more focused. **How we respond to the small challenges in life dictates how we respond to the big ones. If we can recover from small failures with energy, positivity, and integrity, we will be able to do the same when we face failures in our jobs, in our relationships, and in our lives.**

CREATING CULTURE

We are constantly reinventing ourselves. The question is, "Into what?" Are we growing closer to becoming the person God is calling us to be, or are we becoming something . . . else? True reinvention doesn't mean changing who you are; it means discovering the person you've always been.

Find a truth-teller. Whom can you trust to tell you the hard things you need to hear?

Listen to your body. What is your body doing when you talk? Is your body language communicating the message you want?

Tell a story. What personal reinvention stories do you share with others? What do those stories tell people about you?

Be a truth-teller. When have you had to tell someone a hard truth? How did you let that person know that you cared, that you weren't putting him or her down?

5

FIND A WAY

After graduating from Creighton, I knew what I wanted next: I wanted to be a head basketball coach at a Division I school. But I also knew I couldn't just jump straight into doing that; I had to find a way to get there. I had to apply my energy and resiliency to realize my vision. Sometimes this required me to take advantage of opportunities that presented themselves, and other times I had to get creative to make my own opportunities.

In 1991, Tony Barone left Creighton to become the head coach at Texas A&M. I had been a volunteer assistant under him at Creighton, and I wanted to follow him and be his restricted-earnings coach. It would mean a low salary for me, but I would get to continue to work with and learn from him. Coach Barone had been in College Station for a week, preparing to take over the program, and was coming back to Omaha. Since there were no direct flights between College Station and Omaha, Mrs. Barone had to drive the two-plus hours to the Kansas City airport to pick him up.

"Can I do it?" I asked.

"What do you mean?"

"Let me pick him up," I explained. "That will give me two and a half hours to drive with him and have his ear."

Mrs. B. (everyone on the team and staff called Kathy Barone "Mrs. B.") said yes, and I went to Kansas City to pick up Coach. On our ride back to Omaha, I made my case. I told him why he should take me to Texas A&M as his restricted-earnings coach: I was a former player, I could sell his culture, I believed in his philosophy, and I understood his system. I succeeded. He hired me, and I was the only assistant from his staff at Creighton whom he took with him to Texas A&M.

I did something similar to get the head coaching job at UALR. I had been an assistant under head coach Sidney Moncrief during the 1999–2000 season. I was interviewing for an assistant coaching position at Wake Forest when Sidney made the surprise announcement that he was leaving to become an assistant coach with the Dallas Mavericks. My mind was racing. I landed at the airport in Little Rock at 10:30 p.m. Knowing that the athletic director would be in his office late, I went straight in. I didn't wait until the next morning or for them to reach out to me. I marched into his office and told him why he should hire me—a thirty-one-year-old assistant coach with no head coaching experience—to be the next head coach. He told me that it was going to be a long process. I told him I would do whatever it took for as long as it took. When I met with the head of the search committee, I told him that I was going to make it hard for them not to hire me. I got the job, and at thirty-one years old, I became one of the youngest head basketball coaches in Division I.

When I was in my fourth year as an assistant for Rick Majerus, I got a call from an executive recruiter at a well-known search firm. A Division I school in Texas had just fired their coach. This university wanted to hire a new head coach as soon as possible, and I was at the top of their list. The recruiter of the search firm asked me if I was interested in the job.

"Yeah," I said, "I want to be a head coach again."

But as I was going through the interview process, I kept wondering if I really wanted that job. My wife and I had built a great life where we were. And the program at Saint Louis University was on the rise. We had built the program and were going to be strong the next year. But still, I wanted to be a head coach.

I had a phone interview with this school in South Texas, and I was invited to Dallas for an in-person interview with the university president and the athletic director. We had set up the interview for a Friday. As the week went on, I kept wondering, "Do I really want to do this?"

On the Wednesday before the interview, my agent called to talk about a new job opportunity that had opened up at Loyola University Chicago. He told me something that most people didn't know: the same search firm that was handling the search at the school in South Texas was also heading the search for Loyola.

I developed a plan. I said to myself, "I'm gonna go down to Dallas and knock this thing out of the park." Not to get the job in South Texas—I knew that wasn't the right fit for me—but to impress the recruiter and put my name at the top of his mind for the Loyola job.

I went to Dallas and crushed the interview. As the recruiter took me back to the airport, he was excited. "That went great!" he told me. "This is gonna move quickly, like in the next few days."

"This really isn't a fit for me," I said.

"What?!?" The recruiter was shocked. "Porter, this is gonna happen."

"What's a fit for me," I told him, "is Loyola Chicago."

"Porter," he said, "I got that search."

"I KNOW!" I exclaimed.

He told me that Loyola's process wasn't going to happen quickly. It would take at least another month. They were going to have ten phone interviews, followed by another round of interviews at the Final Four. "Porter," the recruiter said to me, "you can have a job in forty-eight hours. I can't guarantee anything with Loyola."

"Loyola's a better fit," was my reply. The rest is history: it took time, but I became the head coach of the Loyola Ramblers in 2011.

All of this is to say that when you really want something, you find a way to make it happen. I was determined to convince Coach Barone to take me with him to Texas A&M as an assistant coach. I put myself in front of the athletic director of UALR and made my case to give me my first shot at being a Division I head coach. I found a way to land the head coaching job at Loyola University Chicago, a job that was a good fit. If I had been passive and just sat back, I would not be where I am today. I was aggressive, and my mind was thinking creatively to find a way to get what I wanted.

Being competitive means that you find a way to realize your vision. If one path closes, you find another one. And if that path closes, and then another, and another, you keep finding ways to keep going. You don't let roadblocks or obstacles prevent you from realizing your vision.

I'm always telling my guys to find a way to get things done, not just on the court but off as well. I once got a letter from an instructor letting me know that a player had missed class. When I asked the player what happened, he told me that he was late for class and had forgotten his ID, which he needed to get into the building. So, he went back to his apartment. He told me he would make up the class. I told him, "There are a million ways you could have gotten into that building. You've gotta find a way." We talked about what he could have done: after getting back to his apartment, he could have grabbed his ID and gone to class (better to be late than to miss it altogether). He could have found another student to let him in; he could have called a roommate to bring him his ID. He had options—it was a matter of finding a way and following through.

In Chapter 1, I talked about Eric Thomas's message about the power of grinding: **your *want* must be greater than the reasons not to do something. When your *want* is greater than how you feel—or when your *want* is greater than the reasons not to do something—you'll find a way.** I had to find a way to get in front of Coach Barone and tell him why he should hire me as his assistant. I had to find a way to get in front of the people at Little Rock to sell myself. I had to find a way to get myself in front of that search firm that had the Loyola job. Finding a way is all about getting creative; it's about discovering that inner source of inspiration, your *want*. I remind my players about this all the time: find a way to reach your goals. You have options. You must find a way!

When I spoke to the leadership team of Northwestern Mutual, I shared a thought experiment I had learned from Doug Collins (who was the first overall pick in the 1973 NBA draft and the former coach of a number of NBA teams, including the Chicago Bulls): What is more important—getting on a bus and knowing exactly where you're going but not being able to pick the people who are on the bus or getting to pick the right people to be on the bus but not knowing your destination? Obviously, whom you have on the bus is more important. **When you have the right people around you, you are going to find a way to get wherever it is you want to go. But if you get the wrong people on the bus, there can be infighting and detours, and you might never get to your destination.**

When I was still coaching at Illinois State, I had lunch with Doug at Biaggi's, an Italian restaurant in Bloomington. He explained that some people have what he called "selective competitiveness." They do something when it feels good. They're moody with their competitiveness; they'll find a way when it suits them. True competitors, however, aren't selective; they'll find a way no matter the circumstances. When dealing with players who have selective competitiveness, you can ask them to think about three things:

- What will you do without a coach pushing you? Will you push yourself?

- How will you react when your coach pushes you to work harder?

- Do you trust that the coach is acting to improve the team?

These questions can apply to anyone, not just basketball players. Students and employees can have selective competitiveness just as much as athletes; just replace "coach" with "manager," "teacher," or "parent." If you know you want the same outcome as your coach, manager, teacher, or parent, you're going to keep working to achieve that goal no matter what. You'll find a way to work through adversity. You have to trust that these people have your best interest in mind, or the team's, or the company's.

Successful people find a way, no matter what. They don't have selective competitiveness. If they face adversity, they overcome it with creativity and hard work. Looking back on the stories I've shared in this chapter, I cannot say that I knew exactly how I would achieve the results for my vision, but I stayed committed to finding a way to realize it. My *want* always remained greater than the reasons not to follow through. It was my willingness to do what was necessary, to go the extra mile, to get creative, that made the difference.

CREATING CULTURE

Life doesn't come with a set of instructions. But we can ask ourselves, "What do I value?" Our values can guide our actions, and then it becomes a matter of finding a way to reach our goals. By focusing your energy and passion toward something that is in line with what you truly value, you will do whatever it takes to get there. You will find a way.

Visualize your goal. What do you truly want for your life? What does it look like?

Check your values. Is what you are envisioning in line with your values?

Get moving. The first step is always the hardest. How will you begin your journey toward your vision? Is there someone you can turn to for advice?

Find a way. Once you're on your way, you will encounter obstacles. Are you committed to finding a way through them? Remember, this may require you to step back and reassess your approach.

6

BECAUSE OF YOUR FAMILY

When I was preparing to graduate from Creighton, I had to figure out what I was going to do with my life. I was a business major, and my three siblings worked for my dad. I could have joined them, and I think a lot of people expected that I would. I was privileged to have a guaranteed job working for my dad's company, making good money, right after college. At my graduation, I told my dad that I wanted to go into coaching.

"How much money are you going to make?" he asked.

"Well, my first year, zero." I told him I was going to be a volunteer assistant under Coach Barone and bartend at night to make money.

"Is this what you want to do? Do you love it?"

"Yeah," I said. "This is what I want to do."

"You gotta go for what you're passionate about. I'm passionate about my company, about running my business. That might not be your passion. So, if this is your passion, then you gotta go for it," he told me.

His answer meant so much to me. He and my mom were the most influential people in my life. **To have my dad's blessing was powerful; it was freeing. His blessing let me know that I had to follow my passion, and that's a lesson I carry with me to this day.**

I like to say that you are who you are because of your parents. I was blessed that I grew up with loving parents who each taught me different lessons. My dad taught me the importance of having a good work ethic and the importance of community, while my mom taught me the importance of positivity and being a person for others. And together, they both taught me the importance of family.

I grew up in Naperville, Illinois—a western suburb of Chicago—where my dad, Jim Moser, was well known. He owned Moser Lumber and Moser Enterprises. The Moser name was a big name in Naperville, and we were fortunate to have the resources to do a lot. But my dad would not let me, my brothers, or my sister feel that we were entitled to anything. He wouldn't let me walk around like I owned the town and do whatever I wanted. He wouldn't let me drive the biggest car, even though they had the resources to get me any car I wanted. (I drove around in a beater that made me feel like Fred Flintstone because it felt like I had to use my feet to get it started.) He had me working in the lumber yard when I was fifteen years old. On my first day, my dad told the guys, all of whom were union, "Work him to the bone." I know he told them to work me harder because I was his son. One time, a semitruck with a trailer full of insulation had just arrived, and the foreman said to me, "Porter, start unloading the bales of insulation. We need it unloaded by noon."

The bales were stacked on pallets, so I'd reach around a bale of insulation and move it from the trailer to the shed in the lumber yard. After an hour and a half, my dad and the foreman came to check on me. I was exhausted, my arms cut up and bloody from the insulation—it was made of fiberglass, and the strands of glass shredded my arms. In those ninety minutes, I hadn't made a dent. The trailer was still full. Like a baseball manager calling for a relief pitcher, my dad signaled to one of the guys. He came over on a forklift, lifted an entire pallet of insulation, and removed it from the trailer. They unloaded the entire trailer in about forty minutes. My dad and the foreman walked away grinning.

The guys also taught me how to drive a straddle buggy. Unlike a forklift that carries a load in the front, you drive a straddle buggy above the load, which it carries underneath the belly of the vehicle. The driver sits about ten feet off the ground, and I had to drive over the load, lift it, and drive it into the shed and drop it off. There, the lumber could be loaded into bins. My dad was watching from his office, making everyone a little nervous. I was able to drive the straddle buggy into the shed, out of sight of my dad's office. The guys started cheering. But as I was backing out, I hit one of the bins of lumber, knocking over all the wood. Fortunately, my dad didn't see me do that.

During the summers, I'd be at the lumberyard at six a.m. and work until three p.m. Then I'd do my weight training, followed by playing in a summer league. I wouldn't get home until nine p.m. Then I'd get up the next day and do it again. I didn't need to work. We were fortunate. But my dad wanted me to understand that if I wanted something, I would have to work to get it. I could not rely on privilege or pedigree. That has helped me as a parent. Although I'm grateful I can provide my kids with almost anything they want, I want them to learn the same lessons I learned from my dad: success is not something anyone is entitled to; success comes from hard work. I remember when I was in the eighth grade and I attended legendary DePaul coach Ray Meyer's basketball camp. Coach Ray singled me out, saying, "Porter's attitude, his effort, will get him a college scholarship." As I look back, I realize that my work ethic is a separator. I don't care who someone is, nobody will work harder than I do. Nobody.

My dad also taught me the importance of community. He loved Naperville and had a vision of a parkway with covered bridges along the west branch of the DuPage River, which cut through the downtown. But my dad wasn't going to ask the community to help with the Riverwalk if his own kids weren't volunteering their time. So, during the summers, I found myself laying bricks on the Riverwalk for free. I'd watch my buddies take their girlfriends to Centennial Beach while I'd be in jeans and work boots. I remember thinking, "Dang it! My buddies get to hang out with girls, and I'm laying bricks." Today the Riverwalk is one of the most popular attractions in Naperville. A statue of my dad honors his commitment and dedication to building a public space for everyone to enjoy.

At my dad's funeral, we heard thousands of stories of how he helped people. Some stories were well known to us. My dad had given my friends and my brothers' friends jobs at Moser Lumber while we were growing up. When one of my brother's best friends wrote a book, he had the dust jacket printed in green and gold—the colors of Moser Lumber. What none of us knew was that my dad had paid for his college education. We also heard about the time an elderly widow had come to the lumberyard looking for scraps of wood and the name of a handyman who could help her build a fence to protect a litter of puppies, some of which had been killed by a coyote. My dad sent an entire crew, and they built a six-foot fence for free to protect the puppies. He did all these things without ever telling any of us; he followed Jesus' instruction in the Gospel: "When you give alms, do not let your left hand know what your right hand is doing" (Matthew 6:3). I always thought that showed his humility.

My mom, Sandy, taught me the importance of looking out for others too. No one in my life was more influential on how I treat others than my mom. She saw that I was the star basketball player and the popular guy, and she always made sure that I treated others with respect and compassion. At the end of the day, what really mattered was the way you treated people. Just because I was a star basketball player didn't mean that I was better than anyone. She would always tell the story—she even told it at my wedding—about a time when I was a kid and we were picking teams to play some game at recess. I picked the most unathletic kid to be on my team first. My mom would go on to say how that kid's mom called and thanked us, because it made her son feel important.

That was the thing about my mom: She had a unique way of making someone feel special. Whenever I think of my mom, I recall that when you would talk to her, you felt that your conversation with her was the most important part of her day. It's a special gift to do that. I want to communicate like that because it shows people that I care. She taught me that if you can make each person you meet feel important, you are giving him or her a powerful gift. One time when I was in the seventh grade, I came home from school and no one was home but my mom. I was a pitcher on my baseball team. We had an important game coming up, and I wanted to get some practice. My mom grabbed a catcher's mask and mitt and caught for me. I think about how cool that was, because that was way outside her wheelhouse, and I was throwing heat. But she did it because she wanted me to get better, and that made me feel special.

We were always having fun with my mom. She loved playing games: Boggle, Scrabble, charades, puzzles, card games. She got mad if we watched too much TV. "Go outside and play ball," she'd say. Even in the last years of her life, the TV she did watch was the Game Show Network. We would play along with *Wheel of Fortune*—whoever solved the puzzle first would win a quarter. We played *Family Feud* all the time. We'd be at restaurants and make up our own surveys: "Name five sugary breakfast cereals that start with B." I remember when I was a player at Creighton, I taught the entire team to play euchre, one of her favorite card games. And as we played, we talked and told stories. I taught it to the guys at Loyola, too. On a trip the team took to Spain, the guys played euchre in the airport while we were waiting for our flight instead of looking at their phones or tablets.

I play games with my own kids. If we're in line at Great America, we'll play a game like "Who Am I?" instead of looking at our phones. I still play the games that I played as a kid with my kids (and I still try to win). I recently played a card game with my son Ben that my mom taught us called Cassino, and I smoked him. My parents taught me that you don't make your kids feel good about themselves by letting them win. I crush my kids when we play games, if I can crush them. If we're playing H.O.R.S.E. or one-on-one, I never let them win. When they do win, they know that they got me. I want them to appreciate their victories. That's why participation trophies in youth sports drive me crazy. The campers who attend my basketball camps get a participation certificate, but not a trophy. There are better ways to build a kid's self-esteem.

Both my parents taught us that our siblings would be our best friends. Friends come and go, but your siblings are always there. I saw how close my mom was with her brothers, and I think my dad wanted that—I don't think he had that, but he wanted it, and so he promoted that closeness with me, my sister, and my two brothers. I love that they did that, and I do the same with my own kids.

I love that I'm building a similar closeness with the Loyola basketball team and that this family is growing. I have the team over to my house during the summer for a barbecue to help communicate that I see them as family. At the barbecue after the Final Four run, Marques Townes brought Donte Ingram, who had recently graduated, saying, "Look what I brought back in." We hadn't seen Donte all summer—he had been playing in the NBA G League with the Dallas Mavericks. My then-twelve-year-old son Max ran up to Donte, hugged him, and within five minutes the two of them were playing foosball in the basement of our house.

Creating a family atmosphere helps the coaching staff support the players when they need help. We can't help the players if we don't know what's going on. I tell the guys if something is happening with their family, if they're struggling with academics, or something's happening with their girlfriend, I want them to tell me so I can help. I learned that lesson the hard way when I was coaching at Little Rock. A kid was having an awful practice. His effort and concentration weren't anywhere near where they needed to be or what was expected. I lost it. After practice, I met with him. It turned out he had three exams that week and hadn't gotten any sleep. I sunk back in my chair. I felt bad that I didn't know. I promised myself that I would never again not know what was going on with my players. Now, every Monday morning I get academic status reports for each player. I know what assignments and tests are coming up. If a guy has three tests in the coming week, I know about it so I can communicate with that player in a way that doesn't add to his stress. Some of my best players have their worst practices during finals because they are so stressed from being up all night studying.

Each player is different, and I need to figure out how to communicate best with each one. There are some players I can push to the brink mentally and physically, and there are some who can't be pushed that hard. I spend time with my players, get to know them, and understand the best way to talk to them. Some people think that you should talk to all people the same way. That isn't true, at least in my experience. You have to meet people where they are and understand how to push them, when to push them, and, more importantly, when to pull them back. That's different for each person.

The only general rule I have for communicating with my players is honesty. Every year at our opening team meetings, I say the same thing: "**I can handle anything. If you tell me the truth, we can work it out.** If you have an addiction, if you messed up in school, or if you had a party in the dorm, just tell me." I can handle the truth. That doesn't mean I won't get angry. I don't promise that I won't get mad or be disappointed. But what it does mean is that the players will have my respect and my trust. Respect is the most important thing I can give a person. I might get mad at someone's behavior, but I respect that he or she told me the truth. I tell my kids all the time, "If you did something that you shouldn't have done, take the hit. You'll feel so much better than trying to run around a maze of lies." If they tell me that they're going to the beach but instead go somewhere else, the next time they tell me they're going somewhere, I'm going to doubt it. When a person lies, whatever he or she says will be accompanied by doubt. You're always better off telling the truth and taking the hit. Plus, the more you lie, the more energy you spend perpetuating it. That's exhausting. Tell the truth, live with the consequences, and learn from them. **The feeling you get from the respect you earn by telling the truth is so much better than the feeling you get from knowing you got away with something.**

— 🏀 —

I talk a lot about the team, but the basketball family is bigger than the coaching staff, athletes, and alumni. It includes the players' families. When you sign a young man, you are signing his entire family. The parents are a factor in the recruiting process. I want to know what kind of support system a player has at home. I want to know if the values we espouse as part of the team culture are reinforced at home. I once walked away from a recruit because of how he treated his mother. We were at a restaurant, and while we were looking at the menu, his mom asked him a question, and he snapped at her. I walked away from that meal and told my assistants to put the recruit on the next bus—his visit was over. If someone can't treat his or her parents with respect, then they are not going to fit into the culture we are trying to build.

I don't want parents who are overwhelming or overbearing. I've watched parents at AAU games scream at the coaches, scream at the officials, and scream at their kids. I think, "I'm not recruiting that kid." That's not what our program's about. I tell parents right away, "If you have a problem with your son's mental, physical, emotional, or spiritual health, if you are concerned with his academics, you can reach me 24/7. But if you're concerned about playing time, lose my number." Some coaches don't mind if parents hound them about their kid's playing time, but I do. I am proud and grateful that we have the best group of players' parents, past and present. It's awesome to see parents of players who've graduated still attend our games. The lifelong relationship between the program and the players' families is key to our culture.

When I first got the job at Loyola, I visited Joe Crisman, a recruit who signed under the previous head coach. I asked him, "How do you feel playing for a different coach than the one who recruited you? What're your thoughts?" And I'll never forget his parents looking at him and saying, "Joe, answer the man." And he did. Joe was eighteen years old and could speak for himself. He became a cornerstone for our culture, a model of a player with character and toughness. That was a teachable moment for me. I do the same with my own kids. A few years ago, I was on the beach for the Fourth of July with my kids, and someone asked them what their favorite part of the holiday was. I let my kids answer. Kids learn to communicate by answering for themselves questions that are directed to them. When parents answer for their kids, they aren't allowing their child to learn. I've had recruiting visits where parents do 98 percent of the talking, even when I'm asking the recruit questions directly. That's a red flag.

I like seeing how a recruit approaches practice and treats his teammates. If he's always yelling at his teammates, that bothers me. I'm turned off by a point guard who hangs his head or gets frustrated after passing the ball that gets dropped. That player cares only about himself. On the other hand, I love the point guard who consoles and encourages a teammate who dropped a pass. I love players who try to make their teammates better.

I talk to head coaches and assistant coaches about the intangibles such as toughness, work ethic, coachability, and character. I know how hard it can be to drive home the importance of a strong work ethic. I teach this by setting expectations and holding people accountable. When my son Jake was too old for my basketball camp, he would go to the camp at his high school, Loyola Academy. They lifted weights until about noon. My camp lasted until 3:30 p.m.; I'd have him take the train to Loyola to help me with my camps. **You instill a work**

ethic by reminding people that they are not entitled to anything because of who they are or what they've done.

As I said earlier, our team rule is "No complaining, no excuses, no entitlement," and I am big on how the team acts on campus. After we went to the Final Four in 2018, I didn't want the players to think they were entitled to anything. They were getting so many accolades: we went to the Cubs' home opener to sing during the seventh-inning stretch; we were given a skybox at a Bulls game and got a standing ovation; we went to a Blackhawks game and got a standing ovation. It's hard not to feel entitled when you get accolades like that. But we reined them in. We talked openly about our success *and* the need for humility. We said explicitly that just because the team had been to the Final Four, they were not to walk around campus thinking they owned God's green earth. We told them, "This is great. But it doesn't change who we are or what we're about." It's a credit to those players that they believed in the "No excuses, no complaining, no entitlement" motto. I am proud of how they handled themselves. On freshman move-in day, the guys were helping carry students' stuff into the dorm rooms. They weren't too big to be of service to incoming freshmen and welcome them to Loyola.

When you feel entitled, you think that you don't need to contribute, and you don't worry about what value you bring to the table. That's not me. I want to know what kind of value I can bring. In reinventing myself after getting fired from Illinois State, I had to convince people that I could bring value to their program. When I am looking to hire staff, I want to know the value that person can bring to the program. Often people will tell me during a job interview why they want to work for me. "I love Chicago, I have family in Chicago," they'll tell me. "You took Loyola to the Final Four and that would really look good on my résumé." That's great. But I'm looking for certain character traits: honesty, energy, work ethic. I want to know how the person I am interviewing will benefit the program. That's true in basketball, in business, and for young men and women applying to colleges. **Tell people the value that you can bring.**

You know that someone cares about you when he or she looks you in the eye and tells you something that you don't want to hear but that will help you. My dad told me that. When your team culture is like a family—when you focus on building trust, respect, and love—you can do that. I can get after my players because I know that they know I love them. My kids give me a bigger perspective on things; as they're going through stuff, it helps me understand what my players might be going through. The only way I know how to gain that perspective is to talk to and listen to my kids and my players.

I'm blessed to have had two parents who taught me the importance of family, having a strong work ethic, following my passion, keeping a positive mental attitude, and living my faith. I am so thankful for these lessons because they help me create the culture that characterizes my teams and recruit the young men who would be a good fit for that culture.

As I've mentioned, I grew up with privilege. I know that, and I don't take it for granted. I woke up every day knowing that I had a great home, a great education, and great parents. But my parents didn't let me feel I was entitled to anything. Anything I got, I had to work hard for it, and I had to learn how to work with others. I'm grateful because I know what the world looks like for so many people. So many kids know violence or drugs or hunger or poverty. It's not their fault they were born into situations over which they had no control or choice. A lot of people with privilege wear blinders. They can't understand why someone might not have a great education or why people can't escape poverty. They think that poverty is the result of poor choices. My profession has opened my eyes. I'm grateful to see kids who overcome the hardships of poverty and violence, things I could never have imagined growing up. These kids inspire and humble me because I know I had a leg up in life. I'm thankful that my parents were able to give me that leg up, but I'm more grateful that they raised me in such a way that I was not blinded by my privilege.

I've heard the saying, the older you get, the smarter your parents seem to be. When I think of my parents, I am filled with gratitude for the lessons and opportunities they gave me over the years. During Loyola's Final Four run, my brother Mitch sent me a picture of my parents' gravesite. He had decorated it with maroon and gold flowers (Loyola's colors), a sign that read "Loyola Basketball," and another that read "Final Four." I had been dark on Twitter throughout the tournament, but I had to share this photo. "YOU ARE WHO YOU ARE BECAUSE OF YOUR PARENTS" I tweeted. "I know they are here with me!"

CREATING CULTURE

We are all connected in some way. Understanding that can be a great strength; it helps us discover whom we can turn to when we need help. It also carries with it the responsibility to help people when they need it.

We are family. We are all part of a family of some kind. There are the families we are born into, the families we choose, and the families we build. Who are the members of your family?

Surround yourself with people who care. Who can look you in the eye and tell you things you don't want to hear?

You are who you are because of your family. What lessons did your parents or another close relative teach you? How do you pass on those lessons to others?

Bring value. What value do you bring to your team, your employer, or any other organization you are part of?

7

LEARN FROM YOUR MENTORS

When I was an assistant coach, one of the boxes I wanted to check off whenever I was interviewing for a new job was that I would be able to learn from my new boss. After the 1997–1998 season, I interviewed for two different assistant coaching jobs. The first interview was with another Division I school in Illinois, and the other was with UALR. Both jobs had their appeal. The job in Illinois would bring me home to where I had friends and family; UALR offered me the chance to work for Wimp Sanderson, a legendary coach. (Wimp had been to the NCAA Tournament ten times, appearing six times in the Sweet 16; he had won five SEC tournament championships at Alabama, winning the SEC in 1987; and he was the SEC coach of the year for three consecutive years). When I thought about the opportunity to work with Wimp at UALR, I said to myself, "Oh my God, I'm gonna learn from this guy." I chose UALR.

I only worked with Wimp for a year before he retired, but something he said stuck with me: "I'll never forget that I was an assistant coach for seventeen years before I became a head coach." That is something that I carry with me as a head coach.

A lot of coaches, especially early in their careers, might want to coach at schools that have great name recognition or pay good money. That was never the most important factor for me. I chose places where I knew I would be able to learn, not just about the game but also about life. What I took from my time with Wimp was that I must always remember what it was like to be an assistant coach and to appreciate the job I had. I've been fortunate to continue to grow in wisdom, learning from mentors throughout my career.

I know that I always need to learn more. I am obsessed with getting better. I tell my players that I love studying successful people in all walks of life. You can learn so much from them because they each reveal reasons why some people are successful and some aren't, why some teams win and some don't. I like catchy phrases that I read or hear, and I jot them down so I don't forget. One of them is "Be a life-long learner," which I learned from longtime college and NBA coach Kevin Eastman. I need to constantly improve. The game is always evolving; I'm excited to see how it evolves, and I want to evolve with it. I have boxes filled with notes from books I've read and speeches I've heard that have really helped me. I want to continue to meet new people and new coaches and learn from them, just as I've learned from the two men who were among the most important mentors in my life: Tony Barone and Rick Majerus.

Both of them taught me important life lessons. Coach B. taught me the importance of learning and of being your true self when you coach. You need humility to learn. If you think you know it all, you won't try to improve, which leads to conceit and stagnation. A commitment to learning is necessary for growth, professionally and personally. Coach B. also taught me that it is possible to be a great coach and a great husband and father. Work-life balance is possible; it requires deciding to put family first and then finding a balance to maintain that priority.

When I found myself away from home for the first time at Creighton, Coach B. became the second most influential male figure in my life, after my dad. At first, he intimidated me—after all, he was my college coach. He was tough on us, but we knew it was because he cared. Over the years we built a relationship of mutual love and respect. He hired me as an assistant when he became the head coach at Texas A&M in 1991. He insisted that I continue to study and learn the game. You think you know the game as a player, but there is so much more to coaching. He'd often complain to me, "Your generation never had to coach high school." Coaches of his generation had all coached high school before becoming college coaches, and as high school coaches, they had teaching duties as well. They knew how to teach. In the early 1990s, coaches were hired not because of their coaching experience but because they could recruit desirable players. They didn't know how to teach the game, and when they became head coaches, they weren't ready to build winning teams.

Coach B. made sure I learned the game from a new perspective and knew how to teach it. He'd grill me after practices. He sent me to coaching clinics around the country, and every time I came back, he would review my notes and ask me what I learned. He was hard on me, and I didn't always like it. He expected me to study, and he held me accountable for learning. But man, did it help me learn the ins and outs of the game. **Requiring accountability, I've learned, is a sign of love because it shows how much a person cares about your getting better.** I knew how much Coach B. cared about me because he wanted me to get better at my craft. As I look back on my time working for Coach B., I'm grateful he was hard on me as an assistant.

I appreciate the value of learning, and because of him, I am constantly trying to learn new things because he trained me to be in that mindset.

When I was a player for Coach B., he pushed me hard. I mean, he was after me, all the time, making sure I was giving everything I had, but there wasn't a day that went by that I didn't think he cared about me. That became even more evident when I started to work for him. I saw behind the scenes how much he loved his players. On the court, he held them to high levels of accountability, pushing them to their limits. But in coaches' meetings, I saw the passion and love he had for his players.

I saw such a different side of him working for him, and we became close. The older I got and the more I worked with him, the more I saw what an amazing man he was. Coach B. even read one of the readings at my wedding. When he went up to read, he stopped and said, "I know this is not part of the Catholic tradition, but I'm going to do it my way." And he proceeded to say some beautiful things about Megan and me and how we found each other. Then he read the reading.

Coach B. taught me about family and balance. Megan and I still talk about a sign the Barones had in their kitchen: "We interrupt this marriage for the basketball season." It was a great example of using humor to break the tension. On the day Coach B. died, I was able to go to his bedside and sit and talk to him. I told him what he meant to me, how he inspired me to believe that it was possible to maintain a balance between family and the basketball court. I told him, "I've taken so many things from you, and one of the things is that you taught me how to have a great marriage while being a head coach." And I'm blessed because I have that: a great, healthy marriage. Coach B. worked so hard at being a coach, but he also kept

Porter Moser played guard as a Creighton University Bluejay from 1986–1990.

The Creighton University Bluejays celebrate their Missouri Valley Conference championship. Creighton won both the regular season and conference tournament championships in the 1988–1989 season and went on to play in the NCAA Tournament that year.

Porter Moser kneels at center, to the left of the trophy. Head coach Tony Barone stands with both arms raised to the right of Moser.

Assistant coach Porter Moser discusses strategy with head coach Rick Majerus of the Saint Louis University Billikens.

Assistant coach Porter Moser observes head coach Tony Barone of Texas A&M University during a game. Tony Barone hired Porter Moser as an assistant when Barone left Creighton to become the head coach at Texas A&M.

Head coach Porter Moser of the Loyola Ramblers looks on during practice before the 2018 Men's NCAA Final Four at the Alamodome on March 30, 2018, in San Antonio, Texas.

Head coach Porter Moser of the Loyola Ramblers reacts against the Michigan Wolverines in the second half during the 2018 NCAA Men's Final Four Semifinal at the Alamodome on March 31, 2018, in San Antonio, Texas.

Head coach Porter Moser of the Loyola Ramblers celebrates with his family after the Elite Eight game against the Kansas State Wildcats on March 24, 2018. Pictured from left to right are Jordan, Ben, Porter, Max, Megan, and Jake Moser.

Porter Moser's parents, Sandy and Jim Moser

"YOU ARE WHO YOU ARE BECAUSE OF YOUR PARENTS!" wrote Porter Moser about the photo of his parents' gravesite, taken by his brother Mitch after decorating the tombstone in honor of the Loyola Ramblers Final Four run. Moser posted the photo on Twitter during the 2018 NCAA Tournament.

Loyola coach George Ireland, right, speaks to his players on the bench during the NCAA Championship basketball game against Cincinnati in this March 23, 1963, photo in Louisville, Kentucky.

President Barack Obama greets members of the 1963 Loyola University Chicago Ramblers NCAA Championship men's basketball team in the Oval Office of the White House on July 11, 2013, in Washington, DC.

Head coach Porter Moser thanks the crowd for their support at the second-round game of the 2018 NCAA Tournament. The Loyola Ramblers defeated the Tennessee Volunteers 63–62 to move on to the Sweet 16.

Porter Moser poses with his senior student-athletes after their graduation in 2018. Loyola University Chicago was ranked #1 nationally in graduation rate for the 2017–2018 season.

Sister Jean Dolores Schmidt celebrates with head coach Porter Moser of the Loyola Ramblers after defeating the Kansas State Wildcats during the 2018 NCAA Men's Basketball Tournament South Regional at Philips Arena on March 24, 2018, in Atlanta, Georgia. Loyola defeated Kansas State 78–62.

Head coach Porter Moser congratulates guard Ben Richardson in the second half of Loyola-Chicago's Elite Eight game against the Kansas State Wildcats during the 2018 NCAA Tournament. Richardson scored a career-high 23 points in that game.

Loyola Ramblers' head coach Porter Moser cuts down the net after the Elite Eight game against the Kansas State Wildcats at Philips Arena on March 24, 2018, in Atlanta, Georgia. Loyola-Chicago won 78–62 to advance to the Final Four.

The Loyola Ramblers celebrate after the Elite Eight game against the Kansas State Wildcats at Philips Arena on March 24, 2018, in Atlanta, Georgia.

his priorities straight to have an unbelievable marriage with his wife, Kathy. (As I mentioned earlier, while I was a player at Creighton, she was the team mom, and we all called her Mrs. B.) He always made time for Mrs. B.; we all knew how much he loved her. They went to the movies together. After a long day of practice—which started with early-morning workouts, continued through the afternoon with film sessions and practices, and ended with calls to recruits—the two of them would go to the movies. I always watched how he made time for his marriage and for being a dad, and I never thought he gave up anything regarding his work ethic as a coach. At his wake, I told Mrs. B. that I learned how to be a better husband from him because I saw not only how hard he worked but how he always found time for her.

At his funeral, the Barone family had his former players read the petitions. I went first. I got up there, stopped, and said, "Twenty-two years ago, Coach Barone read a reading at my wedding. He broke with tradition to say a few words about me and Megan. Once again, I'm going to take Coach Barone's lead." I went on, "These guys are standing here because of the impact Coach Barone had on us. We've learned so much from Coach Barone and that's what you want in life, to impact people, and we are all witnesses to how much he impacted us as a coach." Then I read my petition.

I've seen many coaches lose their marriages and their relationships with their kids because of coaching. I've seen a lot of coaches live with that regret. Coach Barone taught me that you can have an amazing amount of passion for your job and an amazing work ethic and still have balance with your family life. Work-life balance doesn't mean that you're not working hard—it means you are prioritizing balance. Work-life balance is 100 percent a personal choice. I've been able to maintain a work-life balance by working as efficiently as possible.

There's a great quote from legendary UCLA coach John Wooden: "Don't mistake activity for achievement." The more I've read about successful people, the more I've learned about efficiency. **Successful people are not busy; they're efficient.**

I've made a choice that being a dad and being a husband are at the top of my list. That's not to say that being a coach or a father figure to the student-athletes on the team or a mentor to my assistant coaches isn't far behind. Or being a person of God, for that matter—these are all important to me, and you can have balance with all of them. Sometimes you can work too hard and end up missing life. Some of the unhappiest coaches, whether they have won or not, are the ones who say "I wish I had spent more time with my wife, my kids."

When I became the head coach at Loyola, I got a letter from another mentor, Rick Majerus. "At the end of the day," he wrote, "it doesn't make any difference whether you won or lost. It's the father you are, the husband that you go about being as life evolves. You are A-plus in this regard, and that is more important than being anybody's coach of the year." Hearing that from one of the greatest teachers of the game meant so much to me, and to this day, that letter is a constant reminder of what my priorities are.

Rick Majerus taught me so much. The hardest part about working for him, though, was dinner. He wasn't married and didn't have kids, and so after every practice he'd want to go out to dinner, and that was either to a high-end place like Lorenzo's Trattoria, one of St. Louis's best restaurants, or a fast-food joint like Culver's. There was nothing in between. And dinner was an event. There was no such thing as a "quick bite"; it was a three-hour experience. Those dinners became basketball seminars. He would literally talk ball until he nodded off in the chair he was sitting in. Those dinners were transformative in many ways, but two important lessons that I learned from him while breaking bread were the importance of knowing not just how to push your players hard but how to pull them back in and how to create culture.

Rick was tough on his players. He held them accountable. He would make his players practice until they got it right, no matter how long it took. Sometimes I thought it was crazy. I remember Rick riding a player so hard during practice that I thought Rick would never talk to him again. When practice was over, Rick said to that player, "Hey, I got some extra bagels for lunch; you wanna come up to my office and grab a bagel?" He pushed his players hard, but he always pulled them back in. Rick always made sure the player knew that he cared. When I was a young coach, when a player didn't play hard, I used to hold it against him for a week or so. I took it personally. Rick taught me that despite what I felt, I needed to always pull players back in. I could push and push, but then I needed to pull them back in. As much as I push the guys on my team, I make sure they know that I care about them. I'm not helping my assistant coaches or players if I don't hold them accountable. But accountability must be balanced with love and trust.

The older I get, the more I realize that this approach takes clear and honest communication. Most of the time, that's done without uttering a word. You can be hard on people when they know how much you love them. It can be hard to tell someone a truth that will help them. I tell my assistants, "Hey, you need to improve this," or "You're not doing your job." It's even harder to do that with my kids: "Hey, you're not acting the right way" or "You're not trying as hard as you could" or "Your body language is not good." But when you are a coach, a parent, or a leader, you need to do this. You must tell people the hard truths that will make them better.

Rick held his assistants and himself to the same high standard to which he held his players. We were all accountable for what we were expected to do on and off the court. That was part of his culture, and it's part of the culture we've built at Loyola. Rick started his culture from scratch at Saint Louis University. He didn't try to build it quickly. He wanted to build a culture that combined fundamentals, toughness, passion, and love of the game. And he wanted the right guys to build that culture. In other words, he was building a recruiting model. The more I saw, the more I understood what he was building and what would work, I learned what kind of athletes would fit. In my mind, I'd say, "That's the kind of kid I gotta recruit." Rick always told me to take it slow, build the foundation, recruit quality players. When I arrived at Loyola, I did the same thing. I built a foundation based on fundamentals.

Rick taught me that you build culture by recruiting culture. A key aspect of our culture at Loyola is academics. LUC is a great school, and the team culture reflects that. The men's basketball team had an overall 3.48 GPA in 2019. In 2018, the year we went to the Final Four, we had the number-one graduation rate among Division I athletic departments. I'm proud of that. We were able to build that culture because academics was one of the boxes we check off when recruiting student-athletes. I recruit guys who will give an A effort. If they give an A effort, with the help we give them—every Monday I get an academic status report for each of my players, so I know when and where they need help—they'll do well academically. I don't need Rhodes Scholars or guys who got a 30 on the ACT. I don't need guys who got straight As in high school. What I want are guys who give an A effort. I can handle a C student if the professor tells me that he is giving an A effort; the C I can't handle is when the professor tells me the student is giving a D effort. Over the course of many conversations during the recruiting process, I can tell if getting a degree is important to a recruit. It doesn't bother me if a kid doesn't know what he's going to major in. He'll figure it out. I get that at seventeen years old, every recruit wants to play in the NBA. That doesn't turn me off. I want guys whose work ethic matches their goals, both on the court and in the classroom. That's how you recruit culture.

I am grateful for what I learned from Tony Barone and Rick Majerus, and I want to be a mentor to my assistants as well. I know that assistants will go that extra mile to prove that they are hard workers and not let the team down. I know that they pour their hearts and souls into recruiting kids. (I know because that's what I did.) I also know that I want the people I work with to have balance in their personal lives. So, when an assistant has a young kid who's going to make his First Communion, I might delegate some of his responsibilities to someone else—or do it myself—so he can be with his family on that important day. "Dude, go be with your family," I'll reassure him. "We got this covered." When an assistant loses a recruit to another school, I know that I need to approach him with sensitivity, even though I may be upset about losing a talented player.

I'm proud of the fact that I have mentored assistants who have been able to grow in this profession. In the past eight years, six of my assistants have gone on to become head coaches or the top assistant coaches at other Division I schools. When Bryan Mullins left Loyola to become the head coach at Southern Illinois University, I asked Drew Valentine to step up and take Bryan's role in implementing our defense. "Drew," I told him, "this is an opportunity for you to grow as a coach." I told him to visit other coaching staffs that were similar to us on defense to see what he could learn from them.

I gave him more ownership and more responsibility. And that helps me, too, because I get to learn from him and see what new ideas he comes up with. Learning is a two-way street; it's not simply imparting knowledge from teacher to student (or head coach to assistant coach or coach to player). **Lifelong learning is a shared journey in which people learn from one another.**

Learning is essential to growing in your profession. I'm always looking for better ways to do things, whether that's how to be a better recruiter or how to play better defense. A professional is always hungry to improve his or her craft. Just as Coach Barone sent me to clinics, I sent Matt Gordon, my longtime assistant coach, to spend two days with former assistant Alex Jensen, who was with the Utah Jazz, to learn what they were doing with the post defense. It's interesting to hear NBA players talk about how much work they put into taking care of their bodies. They pay as much attention—sometimes more—to their diet and their sleep as they do to developing their skills; they treat their craft with integrity.

Tony Barone and Rick Majerus taught me how to treat my craft with integrity. They not only taught me the Xs and Os of basketball, but they shared wisdom that has helped me discover what makes me tick as a person. They challenged me and held me accountable. But most importantly, they loved me, and I loved them. Tony and Rick never said, "Porter, I love you." They didn't have to. They communicated their love through their actions.

Mentorship is an important part of being a professional. I want my assistants to know that I am trying to help them do their jobs; I want my players to know that I want them to be successful student-athletes. Right before the start of his junior year, I talked to Cameron Krutwig about leadership, telling him that leaders make the people around them better. I normally don't have that conversation with juniors; it's a talk I have with our senior captains. Cam felt a responsibility to make sure that the freshmen were doing what they were supposed to be doing, and I wanted to make sure that he saw that not as a chore or a burden but as a way to help them become better, especially through the lens of his own experiences. Tony Barone and Rick Majerus used their experiences to help make me better. My parents are mentors because they used their experiences to make me better. When mentors have that mindset, it's powerful. I'm always studying and learning, and I hope that serves as an example for my assistants that they will take with them. I hope they soak up how I've handled adversity and setbacks, how I approach things with energy and passion, how I put my family first and live a life of faith. I hope they soak in our system and basketball details. I hope they learn how to teach the game to players. Most importantly, I hope they know how much I love them. That's how I approach my role as a mentor.

CREATING CULTURE

Nothing we know we learned on our own. We learned it from some-one. The most important teachers are those who help us learn about ourselves, about who we truly are. Those people are more than men-tors: they are friends.

Find the best situation. What are the times, places, and people that have helped you learn? What do these situations have in common? Where do you see similar situations in your life today?

Be a lifelong learner. What do you need to learn to grow in your chosen sport, profession, or hobby? Who can help you learn what you need?

Hold yourself accountable. Who holds you accountable? How do you hold yourself accountable? Do you see accountability as an expression of love?

Mentor someone. Whom can you influence in a positive way? How can you enhance your influence on others?

8

A PERSON FOR (AND WITH) OTHERS

In 2011, my first year as head coach at Loyola, I received a call from a friend in St. Louis: Fr. Jack, the pastor of the church where my family had been parishioners and where my kids went to Catholic school while I was coaching at Saint Louis University. Fr. Jack takes the eighth-grade class on a field trip to Chicago every year (he is from the south side of Chicago), and he was wondering if I would give the kids a tour of Loyola's Lake Shore Campus. It was the least I could do. My years in St. Louis were a faith-filled time in my life as I worked to reinvent myself under Rick Majerus, always trusting in God's plan for me. Fr. Jack was a big part of that time, so I was thrilled to be able to do something for him in return. Ever since that initial visit, Fr. Jack has continued to bring the eighth-grade class to Loyola during their Chicago field trip, except now they stay on campus in one of the dorms. I give them a tour of the campus; we go to the Madonna della Strada Chapel on the lakefront; I give them a motivational speech; they get to see the locker room; and they get to shoot around on the floor of Gentile Arena for half an hour. Once a year, I give an hour and a half of my time for Fr. Jack and his eighth-grade class, and they love it. It's a simple way for me to give back, to be a person for others.

I really believe that part of my purpose is to be a person for others. That term—"person for others"—is an unofficial Jesuit motto, and it's a big part of who I am and what I am about. Part of why I am here is that I know I can build people up, uplift them, and give them confidence. I learned that from my mom, but I also learned it at Creighton and at Loyola, which are both Jesuit schools. Being a person for others is part of our team culture. Helping the community on and around campus has helped us follow our rule of "No complaining, no excuses, no entitlement." I'm proud to work at a school that has "people for others" as part of its mission and identity.

Even though I went to Catholic school my whole life and my mom taught me the importance of looking out for others, I didn't hear the motto "person for others" until I went to Creighton. Now, as an adult coach at a Jesuit school, that phrase has a much deeper meaning than it did when I was a player. Being a person for others means caring for the people around you and the people you are with. It means that life is not all about you; being there for others is a big part of it. A person for others is selfless, does not have a sense of entitlement, and is helpful, kind, and sincere. A person for others does not care about the name on the back of the jersey; he cares about the name on the front—the team and the Loyola community. LUC strongly emphasizes that students should be people for others, and it's a big part of what our culture is built on.

Being a person for others also means being a person *with* others—you let people be there for you. You need a support network. My most important support system—the best one I could ever imagine—is the one provided by my wife, Megan, and my four children. I am a person for them, and they are people for me. It's not easy to rise eight times after falling seven without help. Megan has been there so many times for me; I couldn't have done anything without her. My four kids, my brothers Matt and Mitch, and my sister Kate are part of an unbelievable network of friends who have given me a helping hand when I needed one, especially after getting fired at Illinois State.

I remember how important it was for me to get encouragement from the people I loved and respected when I got fired. They reassured me, reminding me that I was a good coach, someone with energy and passion for the game. Their encouragement inspired me to launch my competitive reinvention process. And my family always reminded me what was truly important in my life. As I mentioned earlier, whenever I hear about a coach who gets fired, I want to be someone for him or her. I'll spend however much time I can spare, even if it's only fifteen minutes, to let them know that things can and will get better. As horrible as getting fired from Illinois State was for me, I look back at it now and understand how I can use that experience to be a person for others. Sometimes I think that's why we have to go through crap every now and then; it helps us develop the empathy needed to be a person for others. Whether it was my struggle at Creighton as a young player, my getting fired from Illinois State, or the everyday struggles that are just as hard but don't make the ESPN ticker, I know that these experiences are great teachers, not just because they teach me about perseverance and resiliency but because they teach me about what it means to have compassion, and compassion is at the heart of being a person for others.

I truly believe that part of God's plan for me is to be a person for others and have an influence on them. I live that out through how I run my basketball camps. These camps are important to me. I've been to other basketball camps—both as a camper and as a camp counselor—run by other coaches and NBA stars. They were there for the opening and closing ceremonies, and that was about it, a little more than a photo op. For me to run my camps in a way that fulfills my purpose, I'm there every day. When I see a kid who lacks confidence, I'll pump up that kid with a "Porter Put-up"—a little compliment that highlights something he or she does well—good pass, nice shot, or other words of encouragement. I create opportunities for the kids to shine. The student-athletes I hire do the same thing—that becomes part of *their* purpose. I tell them that if they see a kid having a difficult time, their job is to uplift him or her.

I went to DePaul coach Ray Meyer's camps in Three Lakes, Wisconsin, every year between fourth and ninth grade. For two weeks in the summer, I would be in the woods and sleep in a cabin with no air conditioning, no electronics, and no phones. The food was horrible. But Coach Ray was always available for the campers. He was there every day, in the same conditions as us, running the stations with us. He knew everyone's names. Coach Ray made each of us feel important. He would even turn the dining hall into a chapel on Sunday for those who wanted to go to Mass. When I look back at those camps, I realize how much I loved going to them. Coach Ray and his camps were such an important and positive influence on my life, and I hope that my camps have the same impact on the kids who attend them.

The first year I started my basketball camp at Loyola, I had twenty-four campers. Four of the campers were my own kids, and another three were the kids of my best friends—I had seventeen paid campers. We ran it for a week at a park down the street from campus. The camps have since grown: in 2019, we ran three different camps throughout the summer, with over two hundred kids at each camp. We've gone from one week with twenty-four campers to three weeks with over seven hundred. I've applied what I learned from attending Ray Meyer's camps: I'm there every day, I make sure I know the campers' names, and we focus on building confidence, not just basketball skills. We teach the kids to communicate positively and to lift one another up. For those three weeks, I am all about the kids at my camps. It's another chance for me to give back. I love that Loyola allows me the opportunity to live that part of my faith.

It's not just the camps—it's important to get young people excited about the game. I'm always inviting kids and their parents to be part of our victories. As the team heads into the locker room, I'll see kids cheering in the stands, and I'll call out to them, "Where are your parents?" Once I see the parents, I'll ask them if they want to bring their kids into the locker room to share in our victory. The parents freak out—they're often more excited than the kids! I do this all the time, but one moment sticks out that shows how big an impact this simple gesture can have on a family.

We had won a game, and, as is my custom, I invited a kid and his dad into the locker room. As we enter the locker room, the kid walks right past me—it's like I'm not even there—and he launches into this victory speech like he was Knute Rockne. The guys are sitting in their chairs and loving it as the kid is yelling with excitement: "You guys did this great! You guys did that great!" He went on and on. I'm just letting him roll because it was his moment. Meanwhile, his dad's standing there with tears in his eyes. Later in the year, the dad sent me an emotional letter. He thanked me for inviting them into the locker room, and he explained how his son had autism, and it had been a hard year for him; he was becoming more quiet, withdrawn, and isolated. That night after they had visited our locker room, the boy was so excited that he couldn't sleep. His dad told me how much that experience helped his son come out of his shell. It was the highlight of his year. After reading that letter, I thought, "This is part of why I do what I do." I read that letter to the team to let them know that this is what we're about. That's what it means to be a person for others.

I get letters like that all the time. I get letters from people who run into players on the street, on campus, or at a hotel during an away game, thanking the guys for talking to them, helping them, and countless other little things. One such letter was from a woman who had visited her daughter on campus. They were on the train when they met Milton Doyle, one of the guys on the team. They didn't know who he was—they just knew he went to Loyola. She asked him all kinds of questions about Loyola, and Milton answered all of them. When they got to campus, Milton offered to help them carry some of their stuff to the daughter's dorm room. Milton was one of our star players; he didn't have to do that. When I got a letter of appreciation from the mom, I shared it with the team. Milton didn't know this woman was going to write a letter thanking and complimenting him. He did it because we emphasize being a person for others. This was a great lesson for Milton and the entire Loyola team. Just as I point out what the players do well on the court during our "Get Better" tapes, I do the same with letters like these.

These letters are victories. They don't go into my win column as a coach, but they are huge victories for our program. I love seeing how my players have an impact on others. I'm trying to prepare these guys for life after basketball, to live a certain way. It's helped us so much as a team to play for one another and to live a life for others. Great teams are not a collection of superstars "doin' their thing," trying to boost their individual stats. A team is a group of people who want to make their teammates better.

You could see our guys live this out during our Final Four run. I'm so proud of the way our guys acted. They were all about their teammates. In the press conference after we beat the University of Miami in the first round on a buzzer beater, Donte Ingram was asked what it was like to make that game-winning shot. His answer: "I thank Marques [Townes] for making that pass. Any one of us could have hit that shot." When we returned to campus after the Final Four run, Marques Townes told the students gathered at the rally, "We're just so happy to bring this back home to you guys and share it with you . . . We did this for you guys, the whole Loyola community, Chicago as a whole. We love you guys!" Ben Richardson said, "I just want everyone to look around and soak this in. This is what we've been dreaming of, creating this kind of environment and having this kind of support and unity in the university and behind this program . . . We're just so happy to have you guys and it just means the world to all of us." This is what it looks like to be a team for others. Our team culture isn't just about being selfless on the court or uplifting your teammate; it's about being a positive influence on campus and in the community.

Off campus, we've recently formed a relationship with Misericordia, which provides a community of care for people with severe developmental and physical disabilities. We help them out, volunteering when we can, and they help us, too. Each year, we have a Misericordia night in which we invite the community to enjoy a game. Just as we're there for them, they're there for us, cheering for us. Our relationship with Misericordia shows that being a person for others is more than just volunteering; it means that you form an authentic relationship with others.

We work conscientiously to build this culture at Loyola. When you're a high school superstar being recruited by a Division I school, the truth is, it's all about *you*. You want to go to the school that's the best fit for *you*. Coaches will try to convince *you* why you should go to their school. Everyone's attention is on *you* as a player, wanting to convince you why you'll be happy at this school and not that school. But then, once you get there, a flip is switched, and it isn't about you anymore. It's about the team. That can be a difficult switch for people.

We manage that switch by talking about it up front. In addition to talking about the recruits—why Loyola's a good fit for them, what they will get out of Loyola—I also tell recruits that it's not all about them: By choosing Loyola, they are becoming part of something bigger than themselves. I tell them about my experience at Creighton; we had been picked to come in last place, but we ended up winning the Missouri Valley Conference and going to the NCAA Tournament. We did this because we believed in one another. I tell them about the lifelong relationships I had formed with my teammates and with Coach Barone. You don't get that when the only thing you care about are your personal stats. After Loyola went to the Final Four, I started showing recruits videos of our post-game press conferences. The recruits see firsthand what it means to play for others, not for themselves. They see the guys quick to give credit to everyone else. They see what it means to play together.

I also tell recruits about players like Donte Ingram. Donte graduated from Loyola averaging maybe eleven to twelve points per game over his career. Now, if you had asked him as senior in high school how he would have felt about that, he probably would have been disappointed. When you're in high school, you dream of scoring twenty points a game, playing in the Final Four, and being drafted by the NBA. Donte went to the Final Four and played in the NBA Summer League and now plays in the NBA G League, and he did it without scoring twenty points a game. I talk about guys like Fred VanVleet. He only averaged around ten to eleven points per game in college at

Wichita State. Yet he was the MVP of our conference, he went to the Final Four in 2013, and in 2019 he won an NBA championship playing for the Toronto Raptors. These stories show young men that success isn't about the numbers, it's about their impact. For kids in high school, it's all about the points. I get that—I was a young player too, but I want to show these kids that there are other ways to have an impact than just scoring a lot of points. You can make a bigger impact by being a person for others. Recruits see what our culture looks like and have an opportunity to start believing in our culture before they even sign with Loyola.

Someone once told me that I couldn't do what I do if I coached at a non-Catholic school. I totally disagree. **No matter where you are or what you do, you can have a positive impact on others.** I read somewhere that people see God's grace through the actions of others. When I look back at my life—especially those times when it felt like I was riding a roller-coaster—I see that God had a plan for me. I hope people see God's grace through me in the way I build people up, make time for them, and help them see that they are part of something bigger than themselves. That's how I give glory to God. You can give glory to God no matter what you do. It's how you live your life, how you impact people in a positive way. That's a wonderful gift you can give others, one that may, in turn, lead them to aspire to help others in their own God-given ways.

CREATING CULTURE

Being a person for others is a way of looking at the world that doesn't revolve around you. Take some time—now or in the future—to reflect on times when you put others first.

Have a Purpose. What are you about? What gets you up in the morning? In short, what gives you purpose?

Build People Up. How did you make a positive impact on someone today, the past week, or the past month?

Give Credit. Who has had a positive impact on you? How can you thank that person?

It's Not about You. When have you found yourself the center of attention? How could you have made that situation about someone else?

9

GO FORTH AND SET THE WORLD ON FIRE

College basketball season kicks off with an event called Midnight Madness. It started years ago when teams would have their first official practice at midnight of the first day of the season. Today Midnight Madness is a glorified pep rally. In 2013, my second year at Loyola, we were still struggling to get students to come to our home games. So we did everything we could to fire up the crowd during Midnight Madness and get the student body excited to support the Ramblers in the upcoming season. The Rambler mascot, Lu Wolf, did a dance called "The Wobble" with the dance team all around him. The crowd loved it. After the dance, the spotlight moved from Lu Wolf and the dance team to the tunnel while the announcer introduced me. Nobody came out of the tunnel. The spotlight moved back to Lu Wolf. I took off the mask and revealed my secret identity. Nobody knew—not the basketball team, not the dance team, not even my kids. The guys on the team lost it. They couldn't believe that I had done the Wobble as Lu Wolf. (You can watch it on YouTube if you search hard enough.)

Midnight Madness is the time to get the campus involved in the program. I want the student body to understand that they are part of the team. I want them to have fun creating a home-court atmosphere. When I came to LUC, I wanted the student body to take pride in their athletic teams. Having their support can have an unbelievable impact on the game, and I had a vision like that for Loyola. I asked if I could speak to the incoming freshmen during their orientation, and I was told *no*. I kept pushing, and a year or two later, I finally got permission to speak at one of the orientation sessions for freshmen. The following year, we spoke at all the orientation sessions. We were now part of the welcome routine. I would tell them, "You are part of our team. We could have so much fun filling this arena and making it the hardest place to play." I would (and still do) teach students how to distract opposing free-throw shooters from their seats in the stands. I have everyone stand up and raise their arms up to the side, and I tell them to shout "HEY!" as I pretend to shoot a free throw. During the fall, I go to the student center and the dining halls in the dorms to pass out schedules and hot dogs, asking students to come to our games. The students are a huge part of our success as a program. I'm constantly challenging our fans to fill our arena. Loyola is one of the best places to play basketball—Gentile Arena can seat five thousand people and it feels like they are right on top of you. The students feel like part of the game because their seats are right up against the court. It's super loud and intimate, the kind of place where student-athletes love to play. Watching the student body—as well as the entire Chicagoland region—embrace us was a realization of my vision for this program.

When I was first hired, Fr. Michael Garanzini, the president of Loyola at the time, told me, "We want to win, but we're not going to bend in the tradition of our academics or the type of people we bring in here." I replied that I, too, am looking for athletes who want to be part of something bigger than themselves. I'm looking for students who will respect a tradition that wants to win, but not at the cost of our academic reputation. Our tradition at Loyola University goes back to 1963, when we won a national championship. It goes back to 1870, when Father Arnold Damen and the Jesuits founded Loyola University Chicago. The tradition goes all the way back to the sixteenth century, when Ignatius of Loyola founded the Society of Jesus with six of his college buddies.

Every day I walk by a Jesuit quote painted on a hallway leading to the Gentile Arena: **"Go forth and set the world on fire."** I love that quote, and I love that I get to walk by it every morning. It is just such a deep statement. It tells me that I need to go out and make an impact. It tells me to have a positive influence on others. I've used that quote in pregame speeches. Those words are sometimes attributed to St. Ignatius of Loyola: what a cool thing it is to be reminded by a saint who lived 500 years ago to go out and make an impact on the world!

We have a similar saying in the locker room: **"If you put your name on it, smash it."** This means that you excel in whatever task you are given. If you turn in an assignment and it has your name on it, then that paper will be the best version of that assignment possible. It doesn't matter if it's a homework assignment, a speech, a paper, or a chore around the home. I tell my kids that if I give them the task of cleaning their rooms or mowing the lawn, they better smash it—I don't want to see a half-assed effort. This attitude sets the standard for our graduation rate. The seniors take that quote with them when they graduate—they say it all the time. I was proud when I heard Marques and other guys bring that up at the senior banquet. That tradition of doing things, no matter how big or small, to the best of their abilities is something they will take with them for the rest of their lives.

Be the best version of yourself and have your actions be the best version of what you can do. That's what "Go forth and set the world on fire" means. It's part of our culture at Loyola. My mentality is that I try to smash it every day at practice. Whether it's leading the guys through drills on the court or leading one of our "Get Better" film sessions, I do it with passion and energy.

When you can set the world on fire every day, you know you have a purpose beyond yourself. **When Sister Jean celebrated her one hundredth birthday, people asked me what her secret has been to a long and happy life. Well, I'll tell you: She has a purpose every day.** That's a powerful thing, to know that you have a purpose, that you have a reason to get up in the morning. And that purpose isn't just to live another day. It's to be a person for others. The world met Sister Jean for the first time after our upset win over the University of Miami. The media saw the guys coming off the court and stopping to hug Sister Jean. That was normal for us; it was part of our tradition. But people in the media were wondering, "Whoa, what's going on? Who is this?" What they saw was a ninety-eight-year-old nun in a wheelchair. But what they didn't know was that Sister Jean was only in that wheelchair because she was recovering from an accident. Months before, when it was a typical Chicago winter—icy, cold, snow, maybe all of ten degrees—she was boogying around campus in her maroon Nikes that said "Sister" on the back of one shoe and "Jean" on the back of the other. Even on a cold winter night, when I had offered her a ride back to her residence at one of the dorms, she waved me away, saying, "No, no, no, I'm fine."

I first met Sister Jean at the press conference where I was introduced as Loyola's new basketball coach. It was my first time on campus, and I went to see my office beforehand. On my desk was a file. I
opened it, and there was a letter from Sister Jean. She introduced her-
self as the team chaplain, and the rest of the file contained her notes
on each player. She told me who needed to get stronger and who was
a little soft; she told me who was a good shooter and who the best
ball handlers were; she told me who needed to get better on defense.
As I was reading her notes, I thought to myself, "Oh my God, this is
a nun giving me a basketball scouting report."

I met Sister Jean in person at the press conference, and she has
been part of the culture ever since. I have received an e-mail from Sister Jean within an hour after every single game. She does the same
for players. It might only be one or two lines, but I've really come to
appreciate those e-mails. Some of the most heartwarming letters I've
received from Sister Jean have come after a loss. In just one or two
lines, she can pick you up with words as simple as "Hey, I'm with
you." Losing can be a lonely feeling. There are always people who'll
be your friends when you win; most of them will even be with you
when you tie. But when you lose, those friends become scarce. Sister
Jean is with us win or lose.

I know she has unconditional love for us; her actions show that.
She's in the tunnel of every game at Gentile Arena. She always says a
prayer and blesses everyone's hands. Her actions say "I care." It goes
much deeper than wins and losses. There's always a line of students
outside her office on campus, and that was before our Final Four
run, when she became famous. Sister Jean has a special way of making you feel appreciated, and she sets the world on fire with it. She
may appear frail, but she smashes it every day by being an example of

how to love and care for others. She epitomizes the motto "men and women for others."

Now, if you want to talk about putting your name on something and smashing it, there was no better example than Tom, a custodial worker at Loyola. From the time I started, I would hear Tom whistling as he came into our offices to clean. He whistled while he worked, greeting people with a smile and a "Hey, how ya doin'?" I'd hear his whistle from a mile away, and I would get excited. I'd call out, "Tom's around here somewhere. I hear Tom. Hey, where's Tom?" The way Tom whistled, the way he approached his job made me think: this is a guy with positive energy and a bounce in his step. I've said in the past, "How you think is how you feel, how you feel is how you act, and how you act is what defines you." Well, Tom was a positive guy, and he showed it with how he approached his job with such cheerfulness. That's how he was remembered at his retirement party. He was a guy who had a hell of a career. For thirty, maybe forty years, Tom set a little corner of the world on fire. He smashed it every day.

A friend of mine said that our team set Chicago on fire during our Final Four run. I love that we were able to connect people. I was invited to a Cubs game by a group of people who had gone to Loyola together and followed the team closely during the tournament.

"That's so cool," I said, "that you've been friends for so long."

They told me they weren't longtime friends—they reconnected during our Final Four run. I heard this all the time. I met women who played on Loyola's 1984 basketball team, and they told me they got together to watch our Final Four run. They've stayed connected ever since. I met someone who told me, "I was class of '98, and we got together with some friends from college we hadn't seen in 20 years to watch the games, and this year we vacationed together." I get chills talking about how our team's run to the Final Four brought people together. That run was about more than basketball—it brought a satisfaction that was different than winning, and I am proud that our guys inspired an entire city. I didn't realize that until after the fact. We reconnected alumni, we reunited friends, and we instilled pride on the campus. That's what it means to be a team for others. And that's why Loyola has been such a good fit for me; it's where I have found purpose and influence.

I am proud and humbled to share in Loyola's groundbreaking history. Growing up in Chicago, I knew that LUC was the only Division I team in Illinois that had ever won an NCAA championship. But I had never heard about the Game of Change, the game between LUC and Mississippi State in the Sweet 16 of the 1963 NCAA Tournament.

In the 1960s, college basketball was one of the many battlefields for civil rights. In the South, the sport wasn't integrated. Some Southern states even banned teams of white players from playing teams with *any* black players on the roster. Things in the northern part of the country weren't much better. There was an unwritten rule that limited teams to only playing two or three African American players, if that. In 1961, George Ireland, Loyola's head coach, was tired of seasons with fourteen or fifteen wins. He decided that he was going to recruit the best players, period. He had four African American starters on his team. They faced rampant racism. They were taunted with racist chants, they had to stay in segregated hotels when they played in the South, garbage would be thrown at them, they were spit on and threatened by the Ku Klux Klan. They feared for their safety at every game on the road.

When Loyola advanced to face Mississippi State in East Lansing, Michigan, the governor of Mississippi refused to allow the Mississippi State team—which was all white—to play the game, citing a state law that barred integrated sports. The team defied the governor—they sent the backups to the airport as a decoy for law enforcement while the rest of the team snuck out of the state to travel to East Lansing. Before tip-off, Jerry Harkness of Loyola reached out to Joe Dan Gold of Mississippi State, and the two shook hands. History was made. (Loyola beat Mississippi State 61–51 and went on to beat the University of Cincinnati 60–58 for the national championship.)

In 2013, the 1963 team went to the White House to celebrate the fiftieth anniversary of the Game of Change. I had the honor to go along. It was a two-day trip, and I was hanging with the old team, soaking it all in. I saw and heard about what they did and what they persevered through—talk about overcoming adversity—and I was so taken by their love for one another, how successful they were in their life (they have sixteen college degrees among them). I thought to myself, "Man, what a standard that is." (President Obama, who is a Chicago guy, asked me how the Ramblers were going to be that year. Without hesitating, I replied, "Young and hungry." He let out a belly laugh, saying, "Good answer.")

The more I got to know those guys from the 1963 national championship team, the more I started to see how hard that season was, not just in winning the championship but in battling through the hatred and injustice. Theirs is a real story of perseverance and resilience. I really wanted to share our Final Four journey with the 1963 team because of what they went through. When I redid my office, I had a collage made from pictures from our Final Four run. I made sure to include a picture of the 1963 team. They are part of our culture, and we are part of their tradition; I never want to forget that. Jerry Harkness, the captain of the 1963 team, talks to us all the time. We also talk about how far our program has come. The young guys today don't know what it was like for guys like Joe Crisman, Christian Thomas, London Dokubo, Donte Ingram, and Ben Richardson, who, just a few years ago, played in front of twenty people. These stories are part of who we are. You need to respect the people who paved the way for you.

When you know that someone else paved the way before you, it's hard to be selfish. **Our culture is based on shared glory,** in lifting one another up. Part of the reason people loved watching the Final Four team was that they loved how we shared the credit and shared the glory. In the last play of the game against Tennessee in the second round of the tournament, Clayton Custer came off a high ball screen, Cameron Krutwig slipped the screen, and Clayton drove off his back and hit the game-winning shot. When we came back to campus, Clayton was a rock star. We had a parade, he was on the front page of the *Chicago Tribune*, every highlight on SportsCenter showed Clayton making that shot. After four or five days of Clayton being in the limelight, we found ourselves in a similar situation against Nevada in the next round. This time, instead of Clayton being open, the corner defender guarding Marques Townes came off to guard Clayton. Clayton passed the ball to Marques instead of taking the shot himself. For a lot of guys, after getting all the glory that Clayton had received, the temptation is to try to do it again and end up forcing a bad shot. Not Clayton—he kicked it out to Marques, who hit the shot. After the game, you see Clayton jump on Marques. We show that clip to our guys to make the point: it's not about one person getting the glory, it's about not caring who gets the credit.

People would tell me that we respected the "purity of the game." I don't know about all that, but I do know that as a team, we didn't care who got the credit. That's the culture we have. We play for the name on the front of the jersey, not the name on the back. Unselfishness is another way we smash it. We don't want to compromise in being men and women for others. Those are the expectations we set for ourselves. The only thing that matters is what we believe about ourselves in the locker room and that we live out that culture of excellence every day, on and off the court. **Set the standards for excellence, emphasize them, and you too will set the world on fire.**

CREATING CULTURE

We are all part of a community. No matter who you are, where you come from, or what you have accomplished, someone else paved the way for you. By respecting the past, you honor your future.

Community. What communities do you belong to? Is it a team? Is it an organization? Is it your family? What are the traditions of the community?

Connections. How do you bring people together?

Smash It. What standards do you set for excellence? How do you achieve them? How do you set the world on fire?

Respect the Past. Who are the people who have paved the way for you? How do you honor them?

10

TRUST IN THE PROCESS

In 2018, LUC was guaranteed a share of the Missouri Valley Conference championship after beating Evansville at Evansville. We had not won a conference championship in thirty-three years, and as I was walking off the court after doing a courtside interview, it hit me: "We're going to be co-champions of the league!" This was something I had dreamed of ever since winning a championship as a player at Creighton. When I walked into the locker room, I was anticipating a huge celebration. Instead, the guys were acting like it was any other game. I knew right away what they were thinking. They didn't want to share the MVC title—they wanted to win it outright. All we had to do to be outright champions was win one of our last two remaining games. Our next opponent was Southern Illinois University. From then on, our entire focus was on what we had to do to beat SIU: play good defense and move the ball.

We beat SIU 75–56. In the locker room after the game, I talked about winning the MVC title in 1989 when I was a player at Creighton. When we won, Coach Barone took off his shirt and tie to reveal that he had been wearing a championship T-shirt under his dress shirt the whole game. As I was telling the story—and as the guys were probably wondering what my point was—I undid my tie and my shirt, revealing an MVC championship T-shirt I had ordered in advance. The guys went nuts! They jumped up and tackled me. I had always imagined doing that as a coach with my team—Coach B.'s post-game reveal was one of my coolest memories as a player.

We accomplished the goal of being outright champions of the MVC not by focusing on the goal itself, but by focusing on the standards and process necessary to achieve that goal. Once we had that objective in our mind, one we could visualize, we focused on our standards of excellence, which included, "Never Quit on a Play," "Show the Hands," "Reach for the Lights," and "Jump Second." We then committed to a process to achieve those standards. That's our mindset: we don't focus on goals; we set standards and then focus on the process to achieve those standards. The goals take care of themselves.

In his book *Win Forever*, Pete Carroll talks about how people want to leapfrog over the process and go straight to the end results. That was an epiphany for me. Obviously, people have goals. Individual players have goals, and I have goals for our team—be in the NCAA Tournament, win a third straight MVC championship. But after reading Pete Carroll's book, I started asking, "What are the standards that will lead to those goals? What will be the process for achieving those standards?" Now, every time I talk about a goal, I come up with fifteen standards related to that goal and our process for achieving those standards. Then I rarely mention the goal again.

More important than having goals is having a vision for what you want. Without a vision, your goals won't lead you anywhere. Your vision is something you imagine or dream of; it reflects your values and priorities. It drives you. And you have to believe in it. For example, my vision for Loyola included playing before sold-out arenas. A vision I had for our 2017–2018 season was for the team to be part of Selection Sunday, the day that teams find out if they made the NCAA Tournament and whom they will play in the first round. At the beginning of the season, we showed video of Selection Sunday from the previous year. We watched teams jump up and cheer when they heard where they were seeded. Being part of that excitement became our vision. It established our goal for which we would set our standards. It provided the fuel for our process.

Our vision guides us in the recruiting process. That's what happened with Lucas Williamson. When Lucas was a senior at Chicago's Whitney Young High School in 2016, he and his team watched the parade that the city held for the Cubs, who had just won the World Series. Lucas had won a state championship as a freshman, and he wanted the rest of his teammates to see what winning a championship looked and felt like. That became their team's vision, and they went on to win the state title. We had shown interest in Lucas for some time—I loved what he was about, he was tough and smart, and he had two state championships. But we didn't have a need at his position, so we kept passing on him. But when I heard that story, I realized that he was the kind of kid I want to coach. He was the perfect fit for our culture, so we signed him.

I used to meet with each player at the beginning of the season and make him write individual and team goals. We didn't do this for the 2017–2018 season. Instead, we decided to focus on standards. We list our standards on our Wall of Culture in the locker room. Here are just a few: "Never Quit on a Play," "Give a Verbal," "Show Your

Numbers," "Every Rep Counts," and "Do Your Job." These standards define our culture. For example, "Every Rep Counts" is a standard about how we approach the individual skill workouts that we have twenty minutes before every practice. We talk about how hard we are going to approach these twenty minutes every day. Over time, these twenty minutes add up, and your skills improve.

The guys are keenly aware of our standards because we are methodical in our process. I learned the importance of this from Rick Majerus. He taught me that if you wanted to be great in time for conference tournaments in January and February—not to mention March Madness—you had to pay attention to the little things and take the time to get those little things right, no matter how long it took. With Rick, we would practice until we got things right. If the practice plan allowed for only eight minutes of practicing a play, most coaches—myself included—would move on to the next item on the practice plan at the end of those eight minutes. Not Rick. If we didn't nail that play down, we kept practicing, no matter how long it took. This is how he emphasized the process. I remember spending two hours practicing against the lane-line down-screen. I thought he was crazy. He wasn't. Rick was holding his players accountable for learning what he taught them. By holding his players accountable, we developed great habits, and with great habits came a lack of slippage. Coaches who allow slippage, or soft focus, in practice will allow slippage in games. Rick didn't allow any slippage in practice, and if that meant throwing out the practice plan until the players got whatever it was that he was trying to teach them, then so be it. To this day, I've never been on a team that had so little slippage come game time.

Paying attention to our standards has borne fruit at game time. We were one of the top two or three teams in fewest fouls. We didn't set that goal. Instead, we worked on specific standards like "Show the

Hands" and "Jump Second." "Show the Hands" means not placing your hand on an opposing player as he drives. That's an undisciplined mistake that results in the ref calling a hand-check foul. This standard reminds our guys to keep their hands in a place where the refs can see them so that they don't get called on any unnecessary fouls. "Jump Second" means waiting until the opponent jumps for his shot, then jumping second to contest it. Otherwise, when a shooter fakes a shot, you jump in response and end up jumping into the shooter, resulting in a foul. These are just a couple of standards for our defense. By focusing on these standards, we became one of the top defensive teams while remaining among the two or three teams with fewest fouls in the league.

You develop a process by setting standards. Then you can take the steps you need to meet those standards, and consequently you'll achieve your goal. Suppose you want to lead the league in rebounding. A standard would be to gain strength. The steps in the process then become paying attention to your nutrition, drinking your protein shakes, and hitting the weight room. Other standards would be to block out and apply the "Moses Malone Philosophy." Moses Malone was a three-time MVP in the NBA, and he said that for every ten rebounds, you might only get one. But if there are seventy shots, and you go up seventy times, you'll end up with seven offensive rebounds a game. The mentality is that going to the glass every time on offense pays off in rebounds by the end of each game. If you emphasize those standards—getting stronger, blocking out, and going to the glass every time on offense—you'll end up with more rebounds and maybe even lead the league in them.

Trusting the process focuses your energy where it is needed to meet your goals. When we faced Illinois State in the championship game of the 2018 MVC Tournament, I talked about the process during my pregame speech. I said, "We've been talking about the process all year, and it's coming down to this game. We're about to enter a forty-minute process. I don't want you to think about the fact that winning the game is an automatic berth. I want you to think about the process of the game." We talked about the standards we were going to hold ourselves to throughout the game: holding Illinois State to below 38 percent field goal shooting, focusing on transition defense, defending every play, getting more than fifteen assists, and moving the ball. Throughout the game, we talked about those standards and evaluated our process. We won 65–49. Thinking about the end goal—the automatic berth to the NCAA Tournament—would have put a lot of pressure on us and distracted us from achieving our standards. Instead, we focused on the things we could control and doing those things to the best of our abilities. We trusted the process.

Trusting the process of setting standards and achieving them has become a standard in itself. At every single practice, I reinforce our standards by throwing out terms from our Wall of Culture over and over until they become second nature. I do this during games and whenever we look at tape, too. If you ask any of the players, they will tell you about the process and how we are obsessed with doing things better than before. I love hearing my players talk about that in interviews. I don't have to sell them on the idea of standard setting; they believe in it.

My team won't believe in the process if they don't trust me. When I started at Loyola, I wanted to get the team to believe in my vision: that we would play in a packed stadium, that we would represent a student body that got fired up for their sports teams, that we would make Loyola a great place to play basketball. I had to convince them that this vision mattered, especially when the results didn't come right away—we weren't winning, nobody was coming to games, we didn't have a practice facility. I worked to recruit guys who believed in our vision, who believed in the standards we were setting, and we created a culture based on those standards. Eventually the guys have come to believe in our process, and that takes pressure off the end result. So many people talk about winning championships. Well, there's a lot that goes into winning a championship—there are a lot of things you can control in making that happen, and probably a lot more things you can't. Part of the process means believing in the standards and building a culture around them.

Now that our culture is winning out, it's easier for the new guys to believe in our standards. The older guys are there to show new players what our culture is about, what our standards are, and that our process has proven results. That helps build trust. We continue to show ways to achieve the standards listed on our Wall of Culture. We constantly emphasize those standards and point out when someone achieves them. That reinforces the standards. That's our process. So, for example, if we were emphasizing "Never Quit on a Play," we might show the tape of a game against Northern Iowa: In that game we were up by one point with 23 seconds left. Our transition defense wasn't good, and Northern Iowa threw an advance pass over the top of our defense. As the Northern Iowa player was driving for an uncontested layup, Lucas Williamson came out of nowhere—he sprinted from half court past three guys from Northern Iowa—blocked the shot, and passed it to Donte Ingram. Donte got fouled, he made two free throws, and we won. Watching that part of the game reminds the team of the importance of believing in the process, of having tenacity, and of how "Never Quit on a Play" is part of that. We never stop reinforcing our standards.

I have standards in my personal life as well. One standard is to be the best person of God I can be. Part of my process in living that standard is reading a daily devotional, such as *Jesus Calling*, to focus my mind for the day. Another standard is to be a great parent. Someone once told me, "Never say no to your kid if he asks to play catch with you at the end of the day." What a great standard that is. I am never going to say no to my sons when they ask me to play catch or when my daughter asks me to shoot hoops.

Another part of my process is to make sure that the first thing out of my mouth after watching one of my kids play in a sport is "I absolutely loved watching you compete and play." I made that a standard after hearing a story about another kid who said the worst part of competing was the ride home with his dad—he knew that his dad was going to tell him everything he did wrong. That just broke my heart. That should never happen. I always want my kids to know that I enjoy them. I love watching them play, unconditionally. I know they are waiting for me to be a coach and say something about their game, but I always wait for them to ask, "What did you think of this?" Then I put on my coach's hat and say, "Well, now that you ask . . ." It is so important that the first thing kids know is that their parents loved watching them play.

Goals are not unimportant. I understand that in different walks of life there are goals you have to hit: sales numbers or deadlines that need to be met, ACT and SAT scores you have to get, grade-point averages that have to be maintained. That's just a fact. I get it. The problem is that people tend to leapfrog the process needed to achieve those goals. My thing is figuring out the process: if I do X and Y, Z will come. Once you know what the goal is, set it aside and begin to set standards that will get you there. Then focus all your energy on the process that will allow you to meet those standards. When you focus on each step of the journey, you'll get where you're going, and you'll get there in a manner that is true to the standards you have set for yourself.

CREATING CULTURE

The difference between goal setting and standard setting is the difference between the destination and the journey. When you set goals, you might know where you want to go, but when you set standards, you begin a journey of growth.

Have a Vision. Think about one aspect of your life—for example, in work, family, sports, or academics. What is your "want"? What do you want to have, do, or become? Have that vision be as clear as possible.

Identify Goals. What is a specific goal that will help you achieve that vision? How will you get to this goal?

Set Standards. What standards will achieve those goals? How do these standards reflect your deeply held values, beliefs, and faith?

Establish a Process. What are the discrete tasks that will help you achieve your standards? How will you emphasize the steps in the process each day?

11

GIVING GRATITUDE

I left Rick Majerus and Saint Louis University in 2011 to become the head coach at LUC. That was also the year that Saint Louis finally broke through and made it to the NCAA Tournament. After all the pandemonium of Selection Sunday, Rick called me and thanked me for all my hard work. He let me know that I had played an important part in getting the team there, even though I was no longer with the program. After Saint Louis beat Memphis in the first round, Rick called while the team was celebrating in the locker room, thanking me again. He called to thank me one more time before their game in the second round.

Rick really turned me on to this practice of a constant expression of gratitude. I remember as his assistant, driving three hours on a Saturday to look at a kid play, then driving three hours back home. Every time, Rick said, "Thank you so much for doing that." I remember thinking to myself, "I just thought it was my job." But regardless of if it was my job or not, Rick made such a big deal of giving gratitude that it made an impression.

Now I do the same with my assistants. I'm aware of the times when they are working hard, whether they have just come back from a beast of a recruiting trip or they have been up all night putting together a scouting report. I remember what it was like to be an assistant, and I always thank them. "Hey man, I appreciate you doing that." Or, I tell them "Thanks for making those calls" after they've been on the phone all day with recruits. When they come back from a recruiting trip, the first thing I say is, "Thanks for doing that. I get that you had to sacrifice time with your wife and family to go to that high school game two hours away to watch a player." Even when they aren't around—maybe they're still on the road recruiting—I will tell everyone how thankful I am for their hard work. I make sure people know what they're doing, how it is helping our program, and that I appreciate their dedication to the work and the sacrifices they make to do it. Or, if during practice I see an assistant make a good point, I'll reemphasize it: "That's a great teaching point." It's something I learned from Rick Majerus. He was always doing that, and it made me feel appreciated. And while my expressions of gratitude may be repetitive, or my assistants may think, as I did, that they are just doing their jobs, they've told me over the years how my words and actions make them feel appreciated. That kind of appreciation lifts the staff up.

Conversely, feeling underappreciated is tough. Marriages fall apart because one spouse feels underappreciated. People leave their jobs because they feel underappreciated, saying to themselves, "The boss has no idea of all that I'm doing." I know firsthand what it's like to be taken for granted and how good it feels to feel appreciated. So why not take the route of gratitude and make people feel good about themselves by letting them know how much I appreciate them?

Sometimes giving gratitude means taking a good suggestion and giving credit for it. When we played Nevada in the Sweet Sixteen, one of my assistants, Bryan Mullins, suggested that we start Aundre Jackson, our starting forward, instead of center Cameron Krutwig. This would be a new look for us, but Bryan thought it would give us a quicker start to the second half. "What do you think?" Bryan asked. I liked the idea—Nevada wasn't a big team, relatively speaking, so we wouldn't be sacrificing anything size-wise by starting Aundre. It worked. We were able to push the ball down the court and make some easy layups. When I was asked about that switch in the postgame interview, I gave Bryan credit. It was a great suggestion, and I had the opportunity to thank Bryan on a national stage. I didn't think twice about it—we're in this together. Later, the *Chicago Tribune* wrote an article about him. I'm sure that empowered Bryan and all my assistants; they don't need to be afraid to make suggestions. I'll recognize them, give them credit for their contribution, and show my appreciation. That helps them become good leaders.

I want my wife Megan to know how much I appreciate the support she has given me. So much of what she does behind the scenes helps me do my job; I couldn't do what I do without her dedicated work and love. We may be out with people, and they will ask her, "Do you work?" When she tells them no, the usual response is something like, "Oh, you're a stay-at-home mom."

"She's not a stay-at-home mom," I'll say. "Megan's a domestic engineer!"

We have four kids within five years of one another. They've all played on travel teams, and we live in an area where "close" means a drive that's less than forty-five minutes away. Sometimes practices are over an hour away, and Megan makes it happen. It's not easy to pick up the kids from their high school, Loyola Academy, and then fight traffic to get to my game. I'm grateful for how she has taken a lot of things off my plate by handling so much for our kids.

One of the things I've learned from Jon Gordon's book *The Positive Dog* is that you can't be grateful and stressed at the same time. That really resonated with me because it helped me realize that gratitude, positivity, and energy go hand in hand. God wants us to have a thankful heart. Gratitude is part of God's plan for all of us. I practice gratitude daily. Every day I write in my journal three things I'm grateful for. They don't have to be big things. It might be as simple as "Man, I had my favorite meal last night," or "I got to sit down with my son and eat breakfast with him before he went to school." This practice puts me in a good mood for the rest of the day, and it's something I can return to when I face adversity throughout the day.

Making gratitude part of your morning commute is a great way to start your day. As I drive to work, I think about things I'm grateful for: "I get to drive along Lake Michigan today." I'm blessed with a beautiful drive to work. I'm weaving in and out of Wilmette and Evanston, I go by the campus of Northwestern University on the way to Loyola's Lake Shore Campus, and half of my commute is along Lake Michigan. Whether you're driving, taking the train, or walking, you can use that time to think about things for which you're grateful. It can be as simple as being thankful for a beautiful sunrise, thankful that there is little traffic, that you made a green light, or that the train is on time—it doesn't matter. What matters is that you are giving yourself that gift of gratitude.

—◈—

When the culture of your organization emphasizes picking one another up, it takes the focus off the individual in favor of others. It's natural to give someone else credit, to say thank you—it's not a sign of weakness. It's a sign of strength. And when your focus is on giving gratitude, it becomes second nature to be a person for others.

I talk to my players about gratitude, about how it makes you feel better and directs you toward positivity. It generates positive energy. Gratitude is how we uplift one another on the court and in the locker room. It's one of our standards and something we keep building on. I'm always talking about giving each other credit, so when Donte Ingram, Ben Richardson, and Marques Townes thanked the Loyola student body for their support during our Final Four run, they were simply living up to the standard that we all live by and emphasize every day.

We give gratitude because we know what it does for others. Receiving gratitude makes them feel good. It makes them feel valued and appreciated, and it motivates them to give that same effort again. My college coach, Tony Barone, used to get so excited whenever a player took a charge—his excitement was an expression of his gratitude. It had such an effect that we all would want to do it again. I always make a point to thank the guys after games for the effort they gave. That motivates them to give that same effort in the future. Leaders set the tone for gratitude. People have asked me, "How do you get the culture to where it's about the 'we'?" Well, it takes time and you have to lead by example. You can do that by giving gratitude and by letting people know that you respect and value the people on your team. And as the coach, gratitude has to start with me. So I make sure I thank my student-athletes and assistants for the sacrifices they make. At one of our first practices over the summer, one of the guys took a charge. I ran over to him, and instead of saying "Thank you for sacrificing your body for the team by taking that charge," I helped him up and chest bumped him. Not only was I grateful, I was fired up! I showed him the energy he had generated in me. He was so excited that he went back and told his parents, who in turn called me to tell me how excited their son was after that practice. That energy and gratitude I gave him made it full circle back to me. That's how gratitude lifts our team up. Acknowledging someone's effort in doing the right thing is extremely important, and there are so many ways to say thank you on the court. Saying "Nice pass," pointing to a guy after an assist, or picking up a teammate from the court after he takes a charge or dives for a loose ball are all ways of showing gratitude. Players see that and imitate it. And that gratitude generates the energy that builds on itself.

There are so many ways to say "I respect you, I care for you, and I value you" without having to ever say those words. Sometimes I'll be in a huddle and I'll ask a player, "What do you see out there? Anybody got anything?" I want to hear what they saw. Heck, sometimes they'll see or feel something that the coaches can't get from the sideline. They have a different perspective. Plus, in doing that, I'm telling them that I trust them. What a good gift you can give someone, telling them that "I believe in you, I trust in you." It doesn't take a lot of words to do that. Simple actions are all that's needed. I may be on a recruiting trip, alone in a hotel room late at night, watching highlights on ESPN. If I see an NBA player do something I had been working on with a player, I'll send him a text telling him to check it out. Not only does that help the player improve, it tells him that I care: even though I was tired, I was still thinking enough of him to help him improve his game.

Accountability also deserves gratitude. I thank my players for accepting responsibility for their actions. I remember thanking

Marques Townes for this after a game against Drake during the 2019 season. We were winning big, and Marques, who would later be named the player of the year for the Missouri Valley Conference, had twenty-four points. Toward the end of the game, he threw this wild pass. I was pissed. It was a careless mistake, and I jumped on his ass for it. Now, a lot of guys might have barked back, "Come on, coach. Relax. What's the big deal? I've already got twenty-four points, we're blowing 'em out." But the team saw that I was holding our senior captain accountable. Marques acknowledged his mistake and took the hit. The next play down the court, he was on a fast break, drew two defenders, and kicked the ball out to Clayton Custer, who sank a three-pointer. Marques pointed to me. After the game, I made a big deal of that: "Marques, I appreciate you being coachable. I appreciate you understanding this."

I appreciate my players' belief in our culture, in what we're about. I want to give them gratitude for living up to our standards and doing the little things that help us excel. I appreciate them for the effort they put toward academics. I know how hard it is to be a student—going to classes and labs, studying, preparing for the next paper or exam—*and* an athlete—the early-morning workouts, the practices, the travel, and the games. I appreciate the stress they are under, and I show that in whatever way I can.

When you're constantly practicing gratitude, it becomes part of your culture. It's who you are. **A culture of gratitude results in an organization—whether a locker room or a company—where people appreciate one another and are happy to be part of something bigger than themselves.** As I mentioned before, our locker room has a rule—"No complaining, no excuses, and no entitlement"—and gratitude helps us live by that rule. If you're not thankful for any-thing, you'll begin to think you deserve it: "It *should* be that way." I watch for that in players I want to bring into our program. When you are recruiting guys, they can easily feel like they're entitled, that they're owed a meal or deserve a jersey with their name on the back when they arrive on campus. During an official visit, if I take a recruit out to dinner and he says, "Thanks, coach, for the meal," that sticks out. It tells me that this is a young man who doesn't feel entitled. When our current freshman point guard, Marquise Kennedy, came for a campus visit, every time someone held a door open for him, he looked at that person and said "Thank you." By the end of his visit, I remembered that.

Gratitude is a faithful way of thinking. I know it's difficult to be grateful when things get messed up. It takes faith that despite the problems you might be facing, God has a plan. That can be hard to remember when things aren't going your way, but if you truly believe it, you will start looking for the hidden lessons, and gratitude will come because you will be thankful for those lessons. I'm grateful for what happened to me at Illinois State because of where it led me. I learned about myself through my competitive reinvention, I got to learn from one the greatest basketball minds on the planet in Rick Majerus, and ultimately, I ended up at Loyola, and we went to the Final Four. None of that would have happened if I hadn't been fired. As awful as that experience was—it remains the worst thing that's happened to me in my professional life—I am grateful for having lived through it.

I'm grateful for the people who have touched my life. First and foremost, I'm grateful for my parents. As I said earlier, you are who you are because of your parents. I'm grateful for the mentors I've had, especially Tony Barone and Rick Majerus. They taught me so much about the game but also that being a great coach does not have to come at the expense of being a good person, husband, and father. I am grateful for my players, because they have taught me about humility. So many of them have done great things and will go on to do great things when they didn't grow up with the advantages I had. I am grateful to be at Loyola University Chicago, to the fans who come to our games and cheer us on. I'm grateful to the band and the dance team—they sacrifice so much of their time to support us. I am grateful to the president of Loyola, Dr. Jo Ann Rooney, and the athletic director, Steve Watson, for having the confidence in me to build a program the right way. I'm grateful to be playing for a Jesuit school in the Missouri Valley Conference. But most of all, I'm grateful for my wife, Megan, and my kids.

During the closing ceremonies of my basketball camps, I give the following speech:

> This is the most important thing I am going to tell you, and I won't continue until all eyes are on me. This camp was very expensive. You know how many kids around the Chicago area would love to be sitting in this college gym, working with our college players, playing in this camp? Someone was responsible for sending you to this camp. My last coaching order to you this week is to go to that person, look them in the eye, and say, "Thank you for sending me to Loyola's basketball camp."

Without a doubt, gratitude is an important trait for me as a leader. It gives me energy and helps me stay positive. I believe that with every bone in my body.

CREATING CULTURE

Gratitude is a gift you give yourself and others. Gratitude makes others feel good because they know they had a positive impact on your life.

Be Grateful. Take a few moments at the end of the day to think of everything you are grateful for.

Give Gratitude. Who are the people in your life you are grateful for? How can you express your gratitude toward them?

Practice Gratitude Daily. How can you make gratitude part of your daily routine?

Recognize Gratitude. Who are the grateful people in your life? How do they practice gratitude? How do they inspire you?

12

DECISIONS

In the spring of 2019, I faced a crossroads. I had an offer to be the head coach at another school in a higher-ranked conference. It was a great opportunity, and the school offered me a tremendous amount of money. I had to make a difficult choice—should I stay at Loyola, or should I take the new job? Everything was moving really fast. It would have been easy to make an impulsive decision and go where the money was. But one of the things I've learned as I've grown older and wiser is how to make decisions based on the things that are important to me.

When I talk about making decisions, I'm not talking about every-day choices like what to wear in the morning or where to go to dinner. I'm talking about choices that impact our lives and the lives of others: what school you should go to, what job you should take, or whom to marry. You will carry these decisions with you for the rest of your life.

In weighing my decision, it's not like I was trying to discern between a good choice and a bad choice. Deciding between a good option and a bad option is relatively straightforward. There's an education process that helps people recognize the difference between right and wrong. Decisions happen quickly, and you need to already have been trained to think about the consequences, about what *could* happen, so that when you are faced with a situation where you have to choose between a good option and a bad one, you'll know what to do and make the right choice.

Education is a part of our process in creating culture. Good decision making is a key lesson in it. We review examples of people who made bad choices and the consequences that resulted from them. We also highlight examples of situations when someone made a good decision. These are teachable moments that help our team recognize the difference between good choices and bad choices, and what it looks like to choose the good.

I talk about this with the team all the time. Their choices will not only affect them for the rest of their lives but also affect their families and the program. We have a bulletin board in the locker room on which we post news articles about athletes who made bad decisions—maybe an athlete got into a car with a friend who had a gun, or he went to a party where drugs were involved, or he was at a party and took advantage of a woman without her consent. We talk about how a split-second decision to do something you shouldn't have done or to be somewhere you shouldn't have been can ruin promising careers.

We educate our guys to think about the consequences of the choices they make, because things can happen in a flash, especially when it comes to treating women with respect. I have a mother, a grandmother, a daughter, a sister, and a wife. I want my guys to understand what *respect* means, and consent is a huge part of that. I never want to hear someone say to me, "I didn't know that was considered abuse or harassment." That's a horrible excuse. We bring in experts to talk about consent, sexual misconduct, date rape, harassment, and abuse. I take the classes myself with my team. I understand that lives can be destroyed by sexual misconduct. There is no excuse for it. And there's no coming back from that for anyone, especially the victims. I have three sons, and I constantly tell them to respect women and not objectify them. I tell them to treat women as they would treat their mom or their sister. And that it better be with the utmost respect.

Not every decision is a clear-cut choice between right and wrong. The choice I now faced—stay at Loyola or take the new job—was not straightforward. This was a choice between two great options. When you're faced with decisions like that, you have to discern what is important to you. As I was discerning what to do, I kept saying to myself, "Man, I'm happy." I loved where I was. I had a purpose. I loved Chicago and the community I was living in and the friends I had made. I loved the parish that my family belonged to. I loved the campus community at Loyola.

A coaching friend said, "Porter, don't run away from happiness." Each of us has different things that make us happy. For some people, it might be making more money. Of course, I need to provide for my family, and the money that was being offered would allow me to provide a lot for them. But there are other ways to be happy.

I was happy in Chicago. Some people take jobs to be closer to home. Well, I am home, and I love that I am coaching a local college basketball team. I grew up a diehard Chicago sports fan. The walls of my bedroom were covered with posters and pennants of every Chicago professional sports team. It was a montage honoring

Chicago's sports culture. One of my favorite posters was titled "Chicago's Finest" and had Michael Jordan, Walter Payton and Andre Dawson—each of them an MVP in his sport—dressed in tuxedos. I embraced Chicago's sports culture growing up, and now I was part of it myself. It means so much to me. I can't even begin to explain it.

I also thought about how fortunate I've been to drive along Lake Michigan every day to work. I loved coming to practice and the culture we've built at Loyola. I liked my working relationship with the administration, my coaching staff, the university president, and the athletic director. We were completely in sync. That was so important to me, and it was another check mark on my list of reasons of why I should stay at Loyola.

After we lost to Michigan in the Final Four, I was asked what I told the players after the game. I told the guys that the more you've invested in something, the harder it is to give up. The guys invested a lot into that season, and it hit them hard when it was over. It was the same for me as I was trying to discern if I should stay at Loyola. I had invested so much blood, sweat, and tears in turning the program around. The first month I got the job, they tore down Alumni Gym, and we were without a practice facility. For eight years, I had talked with Al Norville—a trustee and former player—about our need for a practice facility, which was going to open in the summer of 2019. We had renovated our locker room, and the upperclassmen had really nice apartments so they wouldn't live in the dorms anymore. We were taking chartered flights to games instead of long bus rides. We were being invited to play in prestigious preseason tournaments like the Cayman Islands Classic and the Battle 4 Atlantis. We were going to be on ESPN eighteen times. The investments were paying off.

The more I looked back on what I had invested, the harder it was for me to give it up. And it's more than having new facilities or being on ESPN. We had invested so much in recruiting a certain type of student-athlete and getting our culture and brand to where it is. I loved that Loyola wanted high-character student-athletes. I love the guys in the locker room and the guys I coach with. No program will ever say that they don't value that, but I knew that Loyola truly *coveted* it. Fans told me they loved the guys we had in our program. I saw that in the guys we had just recruited. Two of them, Jalon Pipkins and Keith Clemons, had just committed on the Sunday morning before I left for my interview. Their moms hugged me and said, "We're coming. We're trusting you with our sons." I had a hard time reconciling the fact that I was going on an interview for another job within twenty-four hours of two moms telling me that they were going to trust me with their sons. I thought about what it would be like if I had to tell them that I was going to leave just a couple of days after they had made their commitment. That weighed heavily on me. I couldn't walk away from it.

I was happy that I had found a purpose at Loyola. From my basketball camps to the student body, we had built something really special. I felt like I had connected with the student body by bringing them into our world and making them realize they were part of the team. I felt like I had made a difference in their experience at Loyola. When I was out and about on campus, people would come up to me and instead of saying "Congratulations for a great year," they'd say, "Thank you. Thank you for giving us an exciting experience. Thank you for uniting the student body. Thank you for making Loyola proud." That gratitude was a different level of satisfaction. In my mind, having purpose is impacting people. It's making a positive difference in their lives. And it had been reciprocated. The way the student body had embraced us, the way Chicago had embraced us, that impacted me. I loved that I have had a purpose and an influence at Loyola.

In his book *Training Camp*, Jon Gordon writes, "You leave a legacy by living and working with a bigger purpose. You leave a legacy by making your life about more than just yourself. You leave a legacy by moving from success to significance." When I thought about my decision, I knew that I wanted to leave a legacy at Loyola. I wanted to be part of one of the great college basketball programs in Chicago history. We were on that path, but we weren't finished yet.

At the end of the day, as I reflected on the reasons why I should stay, I felt like we were on the verge of something big at Loyola. When I looked back on where we were when I had first arrived to now, going to the Final Four and winning back-to-back Missouri Valley Championships, I realized I wanted the carpenter to come to my office and add space to my shelf for more trophies. These trophies are for all of us, and I'm still young and hungry for more. I had one coaching friend tell me that if it's hard to leave, it's probably the right time because you're leaving when things are good and people don't want you to go. If it's easy to leave, then you're probably getting kicked out the door. But I wasn't even close to feeling that it was the right time for me to leave.

I was facing a great offer, though. I would be playing in a more prestigious conference, I would be in the spotlight, and they were offering me a tremendous amount of money. I was making a public decision. For many people on the outside, it might have been a no-brainer: I should leave Loyola and take the new job. I had people telling me that I had to go to a certain conference, make a certain amount of money, and keep moving. It can be hard to block out what other people are telling you should be important, especially when you're making a decision in public that people can see and have an opinion about.

When you make a decision in public, you have to know what makes you tick, what's really important to you, because a lot of people will tell you what *should be* important to you. It can be hard to resist making a choice that will win public approval. But the public's opinion might not be in concert with what you want. You might make a decision based on what other people want for you and not what you want for yourself. Pleasing others with your decision may feel easier than making the choice that would make you the happiest. **Sometimes when people are giving you advice, they are telling you what's important to *them*, not what's important to *you*.** That's when you need people in your circle of influence who truly care about your happiness and can help you reaffirm what's important to you.

Something similar happens to student-athletes in the recruiting process. Guys will have a lot of people telling them what to do. It might be their family, friends, or even their coaches. You have to be careful about who your circle of influence is, because in the end, you're going to be the person who has to live with the decision, not them. And that was the situation I was in. Just as guys who are being recruited by big-name schools will have people telling them, "Hey, go to this school, play for that coach," people were telling me what I should do. But I was the one who was going to have to live with my decision day in and day out, and they didn't know what made me happy, how truly happy I was, or what makes me tick.

My circle of influence included my wife and family, naturally—after all, they would be as affected by my decision as I was. But I also included Sister Jean. I trusted her with one of the biggest decisions in my professional career.

At one point, the only people who knew I was interviewing for another job were Steve Watson, the athletic director, and Megan. I asked Sister Jean if I could talk to her, and I told her what was going on. She listened, and I asked her to pray for me so that I could see the right path for me and my family. That night, she sent me a letter that I read as I flew out for the final job interview the following morning. She gave me a lot of questions to think about, mainly about how my decisions would affect others, not just me and my family but the Loyola community as a whole. At the end of her letter, she asked a simple question: "Do you truly want the new job?"

I thought about the purpose I would have at the new job. I know myself, and I was certain that I would eventually get to the place where I would have purpose there, but I couldn't imagine it being at the same level as it was at Loyola.

I continued to pray that the right decision would come to light. I was on the fence, and I really didn't know what the best path was. I was nervous about making the wrong decision, and I asked God to guide me and give me clarity.

On the flight home from my final interview, I wrote two letters to see how I felt about each choice. Both letters began, "Dear Rambler Nation." The first letter announced that I was going to leave Loyola for a new job at another school, while the other letter announced that I was going to stay.

I imagined reading both letters to my family. After reading the first one, I felt that they'd be supportive and say something like, "OK, we're in it as a family. Let's roll our sleeves up and get it done. Whatever we need to do, let's do it." After reading the second one, I imagined my family sighing in relief, "Oh, thank God!"

I got the clarity I had prayed for. The afternoon I got back, I told Steve Watson that I was staying, and then I tweeted out the letter I had written on the plane ride home.

Dear Rambler Nation,

I know that there have been a lot of things swirling out there the past few days. Because I have coached and coached with some amazing young men, and because I have the support of the University, friends, family, and the loyal Loyola fans; opportunities have arisen. I know that is part of the business, but it doesn't change the fact that I'm humbled, grateful, and grounded with what comes my way.

People in the business say that I'm crazy for passing up opportunities and the money. But what they don't know is the amazing young men I coach and the culture we have built. What they don't know are the amazing young men who are committed to come to Loyola and wear the Maroon and Gold. What they don't know are the people and friends that make up the Loyola community. And what they don't know is what makes me tick.

So what I do say to the Rambler nation is . . . let's keep building this culture and making a difference. Let's keep chasing championships. Let's do things better than we have ever done before.

With that said . . . I'M ALL IN!

Porter.

Twenty minutes later, as I was walking through the student union, four students came up and hugged me. Parents of my new recruits called me and visited me, hugging me and thanking me for staying. Where else would that have happened? I had made such a connection with the student body. It reminded me that I was happy here.

Shortly after making that decision, my daughter, Jordan, who is on the women's basketball team at Loyola, came to visit me after a summer workout with her team. We had lunch, and she was gleaming with happiness. I remember thinking as we walked out of my office, "Man, I wouldn't have gotten this feeling had I left." You can't put a price tag on that level of happiness. Had I taken the new job, I never would have been able to spend this time with her. **You know you've made a good decision when you see that the people around you are happy and thriving.**

I use my experience of making the decision to stay at Loyola when I'm recruiting. I'm competing against Bowl Championship Series (BCS) Power Five schools. The guys I'm recruiting have friends telling them to go to schools with big names. These players want to make a big splash on announcement day when they tell the world what school they are going to and what conference they will be playing in. I tell them, "The big splash you're going to make on signing day is just one splash on just one day. Go someplace where you're going to make a splash on game day, where you'll make 140 splashes over the course of your career." Student-athletes should choose a school that is a good fit for them as a player, as a student, and as a person. Coaches face the same challenges. Sometimes there will be a popular recruit who is generating a lot of buzz because he's high in the rankings or other coaches are coveting him. I'll have boosters and fans tell me, "You gotta sign this guy." In my mind, I think, "But if I sign him, will he fit our culture?" I sign players based on how they will impact our team on game day and our school off the court.

When I look back on my decision, I see that I would have made a big splash had I taken the new job. But I love making a lot of splashes every day at Loyola because of the purpose I have. I can say to recruits, "I've turned down jobs that pay more or are in bigger-name conferences, and you want to know why? Because I'm happy, and I make a splash here. I have an impact at Loyola every day. And that's what you can do too." By sharing how and why I made the decision to stay at Loyola, I can connect with the guys I'm recruiting better than I did before.

Having to make this decision was a great teaching moment for my kids. People sometimes glorify money, but money isn't always the number-one way to find happiness. Obviously, you need money to support your family. I was able to show my kids that there are other reasons to be happy. We have a lot to be grateful for as a family, and at the end of the day, what makes me happy—purpose, influence, community, and faith—mattered more than money.

I'm not saying I'll never leave. I'll just say unequivocally, I'm happy, I'm competitive as hell to get back to the Final Four, to keep the program moving forward. I'm hungrier than ever to take Loyola to the next level and be the best version of ourselves every year. If we constantly strive to be the best version of our team, we're going to win a lot of games, and that's going to be a lot of fun.

While I don't know what the future holds or what opportunities will come my way or what choices I will have to make, what I do know is that I will be true to what is important to me, true to my family, and true to God's plan.

CREATING CULTURE

We all face choices that will affect us for the rest of our lives. The key to making the best choice for you is to know what you value, have people you trust whom you can confide in, and trust that God has a plan.

Name the Decision. What decisions do you face in your life? When you look at a decision, try to name it as a choice between two options: "Should I do *this* or should I do *that*?"

Take a Moment. What would be the consequences of your decision? Who would be affected? Have you discussed your decision with them?

Know What Makes You Tick. What is important to you? What gives you a sense of purpose? What makes you truly happy?

Tighten the Circle. Who are the people who put your happiness before their own? Who are the people you trust and who are a good influence on you?

ACKNOWLEDGMENTS

First and foremost, I'd like to thank God for the many blessings he has given to me in life, starting with my faith. The strength he has provided me has allowed me to persevere and thrive in my journey. All glory goes to him.

To my wife, Megan, and my four kids, Jordan, Jake, Ben, and Max: you are my absolute rock. Absolute priority. Absolute number one. Thank you for your unconditional love and support.

To my three older siblings, Kate, Matt, and Mitch: thank you for showing me the ropes and for fueling my competitiveness while growing up. Thank you for always looking after, supporting, and taking care of your little brother.

To Bill Behrns: you are the most tireless and selfless worker, who never hesitates when asked for assistance. Thank you for all the time and effort you have put into this book.

To Erin Estapa: thank you for keeping me organized and sane every day and for ensuring the time to complete this book.

To Joellyn Cicciarelli and Loyola Press: thank you for your confidence in me to write this book.

And finally, thank you to the very talented Bob Burnham. Thank you for your patience and energy, and for sharing your gift of writing to help me tell my story.